clues to creativity

providing learning experiences for children

Volume 2

J – P

illustrations by Anne Gayler

M. Franklin and Maryann J. Dotts

friendship press • new york

DEDICATION

To our parents,
for whom learning and discovery
have always
been
important.

Library of Congress Cataloging in Publication Data

Dotts, M   Franklin, 1929-
    Clues to creativity.
    CONTENTS: v. 1. A-I.—v. 2. J-P.
    1. Creative activities and seat work. I. Dotts, Maryann J., joint
author. II. Title.
LB1537.D63   372.5   74-20622
ISBN 0-377-00015-9 (v. 1)

contents

3

preface

You are reading the second volume in a series of books containing *Clues to Creativity*. In Volume 1 we state our philosophy about creativity and how children learn. If you have not read "Fostering Creativity in Children" in Volume 1, we suggest that you do so.

The remainder of the book is arranged alphabetically. The alphabetical sections A through I appear in Volume 1, sections J through P are in this volume and the balance in Volume 3. Use this book as you would an encyclopedia or the Yellow Pages in your telephone directory—to find something, look under the proper alphabetical heading.

We have tried to make the sections practical. Each contains the basics you need to get started with that kind of learning experience with children. You will not find a lot of theory here (we put that in Volume 1), but rather a practical set of clues you can use to increase creativity in the learning experiences of your children.

Who Can Use This Book

This book is especially for adults who work with children in the church. Some activities can be used with children as young as 4 or 5, and the younger ages are usually specified where appropriate. Sometimes a special section will give a suggestion specifically for younger children. Older children will be able to do most things suggested here, as will junior highs. Some suggestions may interest later teens. This book might also be used by older children and youth themselves, either within an organized group or on their own.

Parents may find certain suggestions helpful as they try to provide opportunities for children to have creative experiences at home. This book could also be

4

used by family groups meeting together in homes for fellowship and study.

How To Use This Book

Normally you will read at any one time just that section in which you are currently interested. Each section contains the basics you need to help children have a particular kind of learning experience. As much as possible, each section has the same format, which includes six parts: WHAT IT IS, WHEN TO DO IT, WHERE TO DO IT, WHY CHILDREN USE IT, WHAT CHILDREN NEED, HOW TO DO IT. Some sections also include: RECIPES, WHERE TO GET MORE HELP, CROSS REFERENCING.

The three volumes of this series contain well over one hundred alphabetical sections. In such a series, all possible learning activities for children cannot be included, so we have had to make some choices, using certain criteria for selecting those that would be included. In general, these criteria are:
—activities that children can do with a minimum of adult help;
—activities requiring a minimum or no purchase of pre-packaged commercial materials, tools, equipment, etc.
—activities that emphasize creative use of ideas and materials, rather than copying or following set patterns;
—activities using materials that are easily accessible and as inexpensive as possible;
—activities that stress flexible use of materials, i.e. using the same thing in several different ways, and
—activities leading to some discovery the child makes about herself or himself, as well as about the world and other people.

Instructions or suggestions for adults are included to enable the leader to open up creative learning experiences for the child. Explicit instructions are sometimes given so that the leader will have adequate background to help the child have a truly creative experience.

One important caution must be stated here. *Always try it yourself first!* Using these suggestions for the first time with the children present may lead to frustration for children and leaders alike. Try out the idea yourself. Learn what the suggestions and instructions mean and what possibilities they open up. Learn what a particular medium will do. Find out just what materials and supplies you need. And most important, be sure you know *why* you are using this activity. Experimenting beforehand will enable you to vary the suggestions and make them fit your own situation.

One other word of advice: this series is not a substitute for regular session planning or curriculum resources. These books should be seen as a complement to session plans and curriculum materials. The many learning experiences suggested here may be used to supplement and enrich the ideas you will develop as you do your own session planning and use your own curriculum resources.

To the Adult Who Uses This Book

You are a special person, as is each child with whom you work. You have your own creativity and your own desire to explore and experiment. The purpose of this book is to give you ideas and your own try-out experiences so that you will be free to let children experiment and explore on their own. Give them a minimum of adult help, so that they can experience a maximum of their own learning. Trust children and their growth processes to develop their own creativity.

We hope the suggestions in this book and the others in this series will help you and the children with whom you work to have many creative learning experiences.

M. Franklin Dotts
Maryann J. Dotts

jewelry

WHAT IT IS—

Jewelry is a decorative object worn on the body or clothing.

Persons through the ages have used such ornaments, often thinking they had special powers. Many symbols or designs used today are revivals of age-old symbols or designs.

See other sections in this series for additional ways of making jewelry: Beads, Nature, Carving, Macramé.

WHEN TO MAKE IT—

Children can make jewelry any time they want to create their own body decorations, whether as a result of studying how a particular kind of jewelry is made, how a certain culture makes a special type of jewelry, or from a desire to create something beautiful of their own.

WHERE TO MAKE IT—

Generally, children should have a well-lighted table-top work space large enough to spread out the materials they are using. Always pay careful attention to the specific requirements of a particular project for materials that dictate a special location or equipment.

WHY CHILDREN MAKE IT—

Jewelry making allows children to:
—create many designs of their own
—explore a wide variety of materials, colors, shapes and symbols
—study how people of other cultures have fashioned jewelry and create their own versions
—create items of beauty that they may wear themselves or give as gifts.

7

WHAT CHILDREN NEED—

—leftover pieces from broken jewelry
—sequins of various sizes, shapes and colors
—small glass beads (to use when sewing on sequins)
—tumbled semi-precious stones (may be purchased)
—paper clips and colored plastic tape
—household glue
—ribbons, threads
—lanyard plastic cord
—old earring backs (cup or sew-on type from old jewelry or purchased new ones)
—pin backs, cuff link bases (probably purchased)

HOW TO MAKE IT—

Check books in your public library for additional project suggestions beyond the following.

1. *Paper Clip Necklace.* Make a long string of paper clips by slipping one into the end of another. Cut colored plastic tape (1 inch width) into pieces about 1½ inches long. Wrap one piece around each paper clip and press it tight. Connect the ends of the paper clip string, and you have a colorful necklace. Young children can enjoy creating this simple necklace.

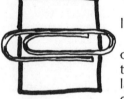

2. *Pendants.* A pendant is an object hanging on a long cord or chain and worn around the neck.

Many cultures have special symbols or designs that can be worn as pendants. India has the lotus blossom, the Ashanti tribe in Africa has the crocodile and Thailand has the swan. Christian symbols, like the cross, dove or fish, can be used, as can symbols for the seasons. Best of all are the designs children create for themselves and wear proudly.

Note: To put a hole in objects for stringing (like a pretty sea shell) use a small hand drill about ¼ inch or more in from the edge. Use an even pressure and do not push too hard as you hold the drill in place. If you make two holes, the object will stay in place and not twist, although one hole can be used.

Sea shells respond differently to the drilling process. Some will shatter, and you should prepare children for this. Plan to have plenty of shells available.

3. *Puffed Animal Pins.* Draw animal outline on ma-

terial, such as felt. Cut out two identical shapes and sew together around the edge, using a running stitch with matching or contrasting thread. Leave a small opening and stuff the animal with cotton balls. Sew up the hole and sew or glue on eyes, nose, ears, etc., using sequins, felt bits, fringe balls for a tail, etc. Sew a safety pin on the back.

A stuffed animal can also be hung on a pendant chain, or two small ones sewn onto earring backs.

4. *Concho Belt.* These belts, designed in silver by the Navajo Indians, are worn by both men and women. Cut aluminum soft drink cans apart, flatten them and cut out shapes designed by the children. Here are a few examples:
Polish all the printing off the aluminum with steel wool. If necessary, smooth rough edges with a fingernail file.

Place each piece of aluminum on several layers of newspaper and press in a design with a dried-up ball point pen or sharpened dowel stick. Work both sides of the metal to get both raised and indented surfaces. The heavy pad of newspapers will allow the metal to give when pressure is applied.

To make the belt, use an old leather belt or a 2-inch strip of heavy fabric, like denim. Hem fabric along top and bottom to keep it from fraying. Form a pattern of aluminum pieces on the belt. With a small nail, make holes in the opposite sides of the metal, then sew the pieces onto the fabric or leather (use the nail to punch holes in the leather also). On the cloth belt use hooks and eyes for fasteners.

kites

WHAT THEY ARE—

A kite is a light frame, usually made of wood and covered with some thin material, that is flown in the wind from a long string. For over two thousand years kites have been made and flown during special holidays and ceremonial occasions in Japan, China, Greece and Italy. Often their shapes and decorations have special significance.

WHEN TO MAKE AND USE THEM—

Children in the church will most likely make kites when they are learning about the people of a country where kites have traditionally been used. When the children want to understand a particular celebration, such as the traditional Japanese Boys' Day, they may choose to make their own kites.

Kites may be flown whenever the wind conditions are right. Kite flying is a good group activity in an additional or weekday session with children.

WHERE TO MAKE AND USE THEM—

Children will make their kites indoors where they can work carefully. Then they will have to go outdoors to enjoy flying them.

WHY CHILDREN MAKE AND USE THEM—

Kites allow children to:
—construct something that must be carefully and correctly made in order to work properly
—improve their manual skills
—experience with real action a celebration common to boys and girls of other cultures
—have fun together with an experience that requires both careful individual work and a willingness to experiment with local wind conditions.

WHAT CHILDREN NEED—

—For the frames:
strips of light wood (balsa, pine, bass or spruce) ¼ x ⅜ inches, or ¼ inch square
balloons (filled with helium if possible)
long drinking straws
cardboard strip (½ x 8 inches)
—For the coverings:
colored tissue paper, lightweight cloth or plastic sheeting

—In addition:

    white glue or household cement
    string (cord, kite cord or fishing line)
    coping saw for wood
    scissors
    Note: When gluing tissue to wood, use many small dots of glue rather than large globs that moisten and weaken the tissue.

HOW TO MAKE THEM—

1. *Section Kite.* This is made in three sections. String four drinking straws onto a piece of fishing line or kite cord and bend into a square, tying the ends of the string together in one corner. (See illus.) Make three squares. (Thread a large darning needle with cord, drop it into the straw and pull the cord through.)

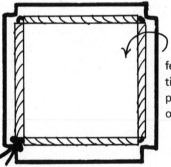

fold
tissue
paper
over & glue

Cut three squares of tissue paper one inch larger than the square made with the straws. Place the drinking straw frame on top of the tissue; bring the tissue up around the straws on all four sides and glue with small dots of glue. (See illus.) When glue is dry, place the three sections in a row (right side up) from top to bottom. Make small holes with scissor points about ½ inch in from the top and bottom edges. Reinforce holes on both sides with gummed notebook reinforcement rings. Tie sections together with two 4-inch pieces of cord between each section. (See illus.) Designs can be drawn on the tissue with felt markers or tempera paint. An animal can be drawn in three sections: head, body and tail. Additional streamers can be glued to the bottom edge of the bottom section.

Attach the cord to the top section as shown in the illustration, using reinforcements and tying the strings around the soda straw frame in each of the three places where they are attached.

2. *Bow Kite.* Cut two sticks (¼ inch square) to the same length, about 30 inches. One becomes the bow stick and one the spine stick. (See illus.) Cut a small notch in the four ends of the wood, and wrap with string to strengthen them so they will not split. (See illus.) Lash the two sticks together about 8½ inches from the top of the spine stick. Attach string securely to one end of the bow and then bend it and attach the string to the other end so that the bow remains bent. The distance between the intersection of the sticks and the bow string should be 6 to 8 inches. Tie a string from the bottom end of the spine to one end of the bow stick, continuing through the notch to the top of the spine stick and down the other side. This will outline the shape of the kite. Cut a piece of tissue paper at least one inch larger in all directions than the frame. Place the kite frame on top of the paper; then bring up the tissue edges, gluing them over the string on all four sides. Leave the tissue loose. Two cords are attached to the spine for flying, one about one inch above the intersection of the sticks and the other several inches above the base of the spine stick. These are joined together (see illus.) and tied to the flying line.

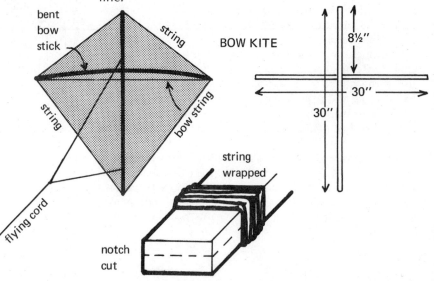

bent bow stick

string

BOW KITE

8½"

string

bow string

30"

30"

string wrapped

notch cut

flying cord

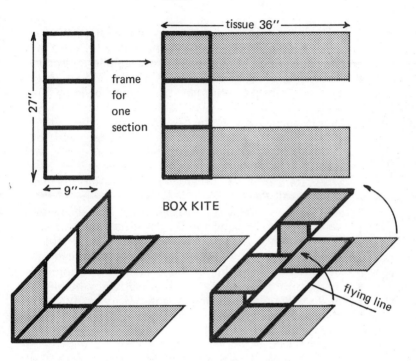

BOX KITE

3. *Box Kite.* In a box kite each side is three times as long as it is wide. Thus, the kite is also three times as long as it is square. For example, a kite 9 inches square would be 27 inches long. (See illus.)

Cut ¼-inch-square wood strips, making eight pieces 9 inches long and eight pieces 27 inches long. Glue together two 9-inch strips and two 27-inch strips to make a frame 9 x 27 inches. Make four of these frames. Then cut two strips of tissue paper (or light cloth) 9 inches wide and 36 inches long. Glue strips to one frame at right angles, one strip at each end. (See illus.) Then glue another frame at right angles to the first frame, making certain to glue wood to wood all along the frames, as well as tissue to wood, using small dabs of glue. Add the third and fourth frames to create the box. At each step allow the glue to dry sufficiently so that the kite frame will remain solid while the next step is being taken. When the entire kite is glued and dried, attach a flying line to one corner of the kite frame near the inside edge of one strip of tissue (See illus.).

13

BALLOON or ROUND KITE

4. *Balloon or Round Kite*. In many Oriental countries, people use kites in the shape of fish, especially the carp, which is a symbol of courage and endurance. The fish kite has a hole from its mouth through to the tail for air to pass through. Use a long balloon filled with helium or air to give shape to the kite. Cut tissue in the shape of a large fish to fit over the balloon loosely. Two tissue shapes will be needed, and they can be glued together and to the balloon inside with dots of glue. Helium or regular balloons can be used. Decorate the fish with eyes, fins, scales, etc. to make it look realistic.

If balloons are not available, make the kite with a cardboard rim around the inside of its mouth to keep it open. Make a circle by stapling a ½-inch strip of cardboard cut to the proper size. The circle can then be glued to the inside of the tissue at the mouth.

5. *Tissue Kite*. Young children will enjoy helping to make a simple kite they themselves can "fly." Each child uses a large sheet of brightly colored tissue paper divided down the center with a dotted line made with a felt tip pen. Mix black liquid tempera with white glue (about half and half), and ask the child to "paint" a shape on one half of the tissue. Fold the other half over onto the wet paint-glue mixture and press down all around, leaving a 4- or 5-inch open slit. When the paint is dry, have the children cut (or tear) off the excess paper around the outside of the shape and stuff the cut pieces inside to give some bulk. Other colors of paper can be used for contrast. Then glue the opening shut and let the children lightly add any other lines with black paint, e.g. wings, fins, eyes, etc. Some children like to glue contrasting pieces of tissue to the outside in order to simulate feathers, wings, fur, etc. When the shape is dry, attach it to a string. Then it will "fly" in the breeze, especially if the string is attached to a long stick or piece of dowel rod.

WHERE TO GET MORE HELP—

Downer, Marion, *Kites: How to Make and Fly Them*. New York: Lothrop, Lee and Shepard, 1968. 64 pp. $4.14.

lettering

WHAT IT IS—

Lettering is the process of labeling, including titles, captions, descriptive phrases, or an entire message.

WHEN TO USE IT—

Lettering is used when children need words to explain something.

WHY CHILDREN USE IT—

Lettering allows children to:
—explain something not otherwise evident
—make a poster, display, picture, etc. more attractive and useful.

WHAT CHILDREN NEED—

—paper (drawing paper, newspaper, magazines, gift wrapping, tissue paper, maps, etc.)
—oilcloth
—scissors, pinking shears
—felt tip pens, pen and ink, poster paint and brushes
—chalk, yarn, rope
—white glue, stapler, pins, sponge pieces

HOW TO DO IT—

Here are some ways children can do lettering:

1. Cut a strip of paper the height of the letters needed. Fold paper into equal sections and draw one letter in each section. The only variations are "m" and "w," which take 1½ sections, and "i," which takes half a section. Fold the paper in half from top to bottom to find the center. When all letters are drawn, cut them out. Try this with several sizes of letters, with thin and fat letters, with uneven and unusually shaped letters.

Use a wide variety of materials: drawing paper,

15

newspaper, magazines, gift wrapping, tissue paper, oilcloth, maps, etc. Other ways of making letters include free-hand cutting, tearing and cutting with pinking shears.

2. Letters may be made with pen and ink, paint and brushes, felt tip pens, chalk, yarn or rope (glued into shape or pinned); also, cut letters from newspaper headlines, use typewriter for small captions, use stencils or guides.

Hints

—horizontal lettering can be read most easily
—use light pencil guidelines to keep letters straight
—size of letters relates to the distance from which the reader will view it
—color contrasts are important; letters should be arranged on a background providing as much contrast as possible
—lettering should help to convey the message by its size, style, composition and surface texture
—cut-out letters may be pinned, glued, taped, stapled, spaced out from background with bits of sponge or at the end of pins.

litany

WHAT IT IS—

A litany is a group prayer in which one or two lines are followed by a recurring responsive phrase prayed by the entire group. The responsive line can be spoken or sung.

WHEN AND WHERE TO USE IT—

Children use litany when they are worshiping in their group, studying various forms of prayer and planning and creating worship experiences in their group. Children can use litany at any place and at any time.

As a group children can pray indoors or outdoors, in almost any location.

WHY CHILDREN USE IT—

Litany helps children:
—form a prayer for their own worship that grows out of and expresses their own concerns and feelings
—express their personal relationship with God through a group effort to communicate with him
—share their prayer with others beyond their own group, perhaps in a congregational worship service.

WHAT CHILDREN NEED—

—opportunities to pray together in a group
—understanding of the special format of a litany
—experience in using litany, either in a spoken or musical type of prayer
—opportunity to see others—especially adults—using the litany format in their prayers.

HOW TO DO IT—

When working on a litany with a group of children, invite each one to contribute his or her ideas. These can be placed on poster paper or newsprint. Agree together on the responsive phrase. If several responses are suggested, the children can decide on the one that best fits their prayer. Print this response on a separate piece of paper.

When all the ideas have been collected, a smaller group or committee may organize them into whatever patterns seem appropriate. When the pieces of paper are arranged in the proper order, they can be taped on the wall or placed on the bulletin board, leaving room for the refrain.

Younger elementary children will enjoy shorter phrases and much repetition of the response. Older children can handle longer phrases. With an intergenerational group, pass out index cards and ask the members to put down their concerns about our world, our lives or our church. Collect these and have someone arrange them into a sequence. These can then be clustered and used as a litany, with the group responding with a common phrase as a leader reads each cluster of concerns.

Responses can often come out of Scripture that is being studied, songs being sung, or phrases suggested by the group.

Examples of Scripture passages:

"Hear my cry, O God, listen to my prayer."

(Psalm 61:1)

"O My God, in thee I trust." (Psalm 25:1)

"The Lord has risen indeed." (Luke 24:34)

Examples of phrases from hymns:

"In Christ there is no east or west,
In him no south or north."

In Christ There Is No East or West
(mission emphasis)

"Come and worship, Come and worship,
Worship Christ, the newborn king."

Angels, From the Realms of Glory
(Christmastide)

"O come, let us adore him, Christ, the Lord!"
O Come, All Ye Faithful
(Christmastide)

"Rejoice, rejoice,
Rejoice, give thanks and sing."

Rejoice, Ye Pure in Heart
(Hope, joy and peace)

Examples of phrases that might be suggested by the group from their own study:

"We thank you, O God."

"Hear our prayers, O God."

"Thank you, God, for your many blessings."

"Help us, O God, to do your work."

Very brief responses will be most meaningful for younger children, for they can often be learned from memory by children who cannot yet read. In a longer litany, more than one major theme may be emphasized. Major sections may use different responses, with each one used several times before the end of the section.

The following litany, given here as an example, was

18

created by third and fourth graders in one class. Each child contributed one line to this prayer, and the entire class decided on the response:

Our friends at church are nice.
 THANK YOU, GOD, FOR OUR CHURCH.
In church we study the Bible.
 THANK YOU, GOD, FOR OUR CHURCH.
When we play at church we have fun.
 THANK YOU, GOD, FOR OUR CHURCH.
We pray at church and at home.
 THANK YOU, GOD, FOR OUR CHURCH.
We listen to the preacher pray.
 THANK YOU, GOD, FOR OUR CHURCH.
In our church we sing.
 THANK YOU, GOD, FOR OUR CHURCH.
We learn of Jesus.
 THANK YOU, GOD, FOR OUR CHURCH.
We bring other people to church.
 THANK YOU, GOD, FOR OUR CHURCH. AMEN.

macramé

WHAT IT IS—

Macramé is the process of creating designs by knotting cord. Sailors were probably the first to use knots to lash things together on their ships. During their long sea voyages they began to experiment with available cord, making items for the ship, for their folks at home or for sale in the next port. Middle East craftsmen also have for centuries been knotting fringe on rugs and shawls.

Children can use macramé to create hangings, belts, necklaces, light pull cords, purses and many other interesting items.

WHEN AND WHERE TO DO IT—

Children can do macramé anywhere, since it takes

no special equipment and uses common supplies. Since they will have to learn skills gradually, boys and girls should do it when they have adequate time and guidance. Macramé is an excellent activity in a camping or crafts program.

WHY CHILDREN DO IT—

Macramé allows children to:
—create new designs
—increase manual dexterity
—create something interesting and useful out of a commonplace material
—experience an old art form with meaningful results for today.

WHAT CHILDREN NEED—

—anything that can be knotted:
  twine, cord, rope, rug yarn, silk roping, drapery cords, etc.
—scissors to cut the cords
—pieces of dowel rod, pencil, wooden chopsticks, clean tree limb or piece of driftwood.

A Word About Buying Cords: Try out several types you have around home to determine which are too fine or elastic and which are too bulky. Use what is available at the most reasonable price. Look in your hardware departments. Chalk line cord is a good thickness.

The purpose for the item you are making will help determine what type of cord to get. For example, an outdoor plant hanger will be most serviceable if made with heavy twine.

1. larkshead

2. half knot

3. square knot

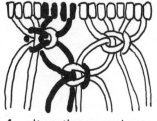

4. alternating square knots

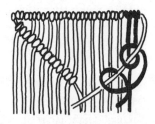

5. diagonal double half hitch

HOW TO DO IT—
Helping Children Get Started

Make up some mountings of 4, 8 or 12 pieces of cord on dowel sticks or pencils, using the larkshead knot shown in diagram 1. Mount a 24-inch piece of cord at the center so that two ends about 12 inches long are hanging loose. For practice purposes use large rope in different colors, so that the children can easily see where each piece is going. Make up a display, showing each knot.

It is important to help children learn to make something as soon as possible, so get them making knots right away. Once they have learned the square knot, they can begin to think about what they would like to make. To make a square knot, first make the half knot (Diagram #2) and then do the second step (Diagram #3).

| Step 1 | Step 2 | Step 3 | Step 4 |

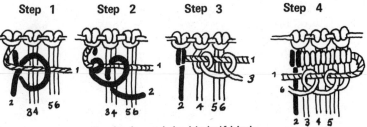

6. horizontal double half hitch

Belts are popular with boys and girls, and free form wall hangings are also good starting pieces. The best part about macramé is that you can create as you go.

Part of the design in macramé is repeated patterns of a series of knots in similar formations. Leave some knots loose and pull others very tight. Make a chain of some knots; leave other cords plain. Help children develop their own patterns.

Only the very basic knots are included here. If you want to study further, look up some of the newer books on macramé in your library. Many are helpful in saying how much cord to buy for the specific item being made.

How Much Cord?

A basic rule of thumb is to have four to eight times the finished length. For example, a belt with long fringe might be 90 inches long for each strand, with a 180-inch piece of cord if you use the larkshead mounting. The finished belt would be about 45 inches —a 29-inch waist plus 8 inches of fringe on each end. Such a belt would have lots of knots and lots of open space. Almost solid knots would take more cord.

Usually you will work in multiples of four strands. Make up some sample pieces to see how wide your finished piece will be with various numbers of strands. Of course, the thickness of the cord will help determine how many you will want.

More on Mounting

The first important step in doing any macramé piece is mounting. Whatever the type of mount, it should remain fairly stationary. Whether you use dowel rods, pencils, wooden chopsticks, limbs or pieces of driftwood, find a way to weight the ends of the wood pieces down so they will not move once the child starts knotting. An easy way is to set a pile of books on top of each end. If you place the mount at the edge of a table, the strands will hang down to be worked with. Some children may prefer to work across the top of a table. In any case, keep the mount firmly anchored down!

Instead of the larkshead mount, you might try one of the following:

1. Gather together the ends of all the strands you plan to work with and make one large gathering knot (see Diagram #8). This will be untied after the piece is completed. To secure the gathering knot for working, put it over a door knob. Or draw the strands around a chair leg, with the knot on the other side. The same idea can be used with any narrow spot in a lamp base, table leg, protruding limb of a tree, etc.

2. A piece of heavy cord can substitute for the dowel rod. Put two heavy nails 12 inches apart in a block of wood and tie a piece of heavy cord between them. Use this cord as you would a dowel rod.

3. A row of nails can be placed in a block of wood, with each piece of cord attached to a separate nail.

Starting to Knot

Before the first knot is made, children must plan for a fringe, if there is to be one. Allow 6 or 8 inches (or whatever length is desired) from the mounting before starting to knot. Begin the knots, using either the square knot (Diagrams #2 and #3) or the horizontal double half hitch (Diagram #6). If you use the horizontal double half hitch, you will create a horizontal row of knots at the beginning of the belt (see top part of Diagram #4). Continue then with whatever combination of knots you want. When you have reached about half the length of the design you have in mind you may want to repeat (in reverse order) in the second half of the piece the design you used in the first half. In any case, be sure to keep measuring your design so that it comes out to the proper size.

Bundling. Roll up long pieces of cord by wrapping each around your hand and tying it with either a rubber band or a plastic twist tie. As you need more cord, you can pull it out of the bundle.

Finishing the Ends. After the piece is finished and removed from the mounting, the ends can be left as fringe. If the cord tends to fray, place a drop of white glue on the end. Another possibility for finishing is to have a gathering knot at each end. Beads may be added as decoration on the fringe. Tie a simple half knot above and below bead to keep it in place.

A Simple Belt. For a belt that children can make, use 4 strings 72 inches long (90 to 120 inches for an adult) of heavy chalk line or drapery cord. Tie a gathering knot of all the cords about 10 inches from the end. Tie the square knot (Diagrams #2 and #3), using all four strands. Note that the two center strands are the knot bearers, and all the tying is done with the two outer strands. Keep making a string of these knots to within about 10 inches of the other end (or whenever you have sufficient length). Tie a gathering knot, make sure your fringe on each end is the same length, and you have a narrow belt.

7. vertical double half hitch

8. gathering knot

maps & globes

WHAT THEY ARE—

A map is a flat representation of the earth's surface or a part of it. A globe is a spherical map.

A globe is more accurate in giving a spherical concept of the surface of the earth. Maps are valuable for more detailed information.

WHEN TO USE THEM—

Young children, who have not yet developed a sense of reality outside their own immediate experience, will probably not use maps or globes much at all.

Older elementary children, who are beginning to have a sense of time and space, may be interested in maps of simple detail. Use the children's own travel experiences wherever possible to help personalize ideas of distance, time and space.

WHERE TO USE THEM—

Maps can be used in almost any learning situation, on the floor, on tables, on the wall, in books, etc.

WHY CHILDREN USE THEM—

Maps and globes allow children to:
—point out the location of a story
—study an event in relation to where they live
—show where they and their friends live
—discover relationships among places
—enlarge concepts of space, distance, geography
—develop their own identification with other peoples of the world.

WHAT CHILDREN NEED—

—maps found in encyclopedias, atlases and books
—maps obtained at gasoline stations, travel bureaus, foreign travel offices and stationery stores

24

—maps from Friendship Press
—felt (72 inches wide) for floor map; smaller felt
  pieces in assorted colors; cars and trucks
—window shade with hardware
—salt clay, plaster of Paris or papier mâché

HOW TO USE THEM—

The following are some ways children can use maps and globes:

1. *Neighborhood Floor Map.* Older elementary students could make this for young children. On two or more yards of felt or heavy paper (72 inches wide) lay out to scale the area around your church or part of town. Draw this first on paper and then transfer to the large piece of felt or heavy paper. Once the plan is drawn, the children can cut out pieces of felt for streets, schools, churches, post office, stores, gas stations, parks, traffic signals, stop signs, etc. Let the children help paste these pieces onto the big map *after* you have talked together about where these things are in *real life* and where they ought to be *on the map.* The children can crawl on the map or around the edges, using small cars and trucks as they live out the activities of their neighborhood.

Older children could make up a neighborhood map for the characters in a story of another culture. This will provide the scene for acting out events from the story. Instead of felt, you might use a white bed sheet or a large piece of mural paper, and felt pens to draw the map.

2. *Map of the Life of Jesus.* This can be quickly made from the accompanying drawing. Be sure to show the location on a globe and say that the map represents a very small area which is enlarged here so that we can work with it.

3. *Window Shade Map.* On a window shade, draw a map to scale. Use the shade's hardware to hang it on the wall for ready reference. Small pictures can be included as reminders of events at particular places. Sketch in pencil the initial lines, then use felt pen to draw the map. This activity will appeal to a limited number of students.

4. *Three-dimensional Flat Maps*. Maps made of salt clay, plaster of Paris or papier mâché on a firm surface may be made by older children to show the geographical characteristics of an area. This activity takes a great deal of planning and preparation and a long attention span. Make the outline of the map on a piece of thin plywood or Masonite or on a tray. Decide on the areas you want to build up and place some wads of aluminum foil or newspaper on those areas. Then cover the entire map with clay, plaster of Paris or papier mâché. (See recipes at end of section.) Tempera paint or food coloring may be used to color the map, and small names may be written on paper and attached to pins or toothpicks to identify places.

5. *An Outdoor Map*. In a large space, a garden can be made to represent an area of the world—perhaps the Holy Land, your state or town. Use mounds of dirt, stones, trees and bushes for the various parts. A great deal of research is needed to build an area like this, but it is a good learning experience for those who want to participate.

Some other hints:

—Since not all children will be interested in them, it is best to use maps and globes as an optional or elective activity.

—To enlarge a map from one in a book, draw a grid of squares on the original map. *(Note:* If you cannot write on the original—as with an encyclopedia map —make your grid on clear food wrap or plastic, using a grease pencil. Place the plastic over the original, using paper clips to keep it in place.) Now make a larger grid lightly on your new material. If you want a map twice as big as the original, for example, make the squares twice the size of those on your original. When you have completed your new grid, lightly draw in the main boundaries, transferring the shape of the lines found in each small block to the corresponding large block. When all lines have been drawn, the entire map can be checked for accuracy, the lines darkened, and labels and other information transferred to the new map.

Recipes

Salt Clay
2 cups flour
2 cups salt
water
In a large bowl mix dry flour and salt until free of
lumps. Then add water in small amounts, mixing to
form a creamy consistency like mayonnaise. Powdered
tempera or food coloring may be added to the mixture, or the surface may be painted after it has dried.

Plaster of Paris (See recipe under Mosaics.)
Pulp Papier Mâché (see Papier Mâché)

masks

WHAT THEY ARE—

A mask is a covering worn over the face or head to
symbolize another person, an animal or some imaginary being.

Masks have been used for centuries in religious
ceremonies and secret organizations to portray spirits
and to please the gods. The use of masks in drama
came about as rituals and dances became part of
the play. In Japan the Noh plays require beautiful
masks of animals and human faces; in Malaya the
Hantu B'rok or Baboon Demon casts spells, especially
on dancers. Many Asian countries have special masks
for funerals. In Africa, masks are used with secret so-
cieties. Girls and boys might research various ways
masks were used in the culture they may be studying.

WHEN AND WHERE TO MAKE AND USE THEM—

Boys and girls can use masks when they are studying religious and spiritual beliefs of other cultures,
when they are broadening their own understanding
of who they are and of the persons around them, and

when they just want to have fun by masquerading as someone else, as at a party or at Hallowe'en.

Children can make and use masks in the classroom, at a party, or in connection with work on a play or drama. Children will also make and use masks individually in their own play.

WHY CHILDREN MAKE AND USE THEM—

Masks allow children to:
—discover one facet in the life of another culture
—portray an animal or another being
—get "inside the skin" of another person to understand something of the way it feels to be that person
—dress up as another creature for a party.

WHAT CHILDREN NEED—

—paper plates, crayons, felt markers
—paper bags (size #10)
—cardboard boxes
—cloth scraps, yarn, crepe paper, pipe cleaners, etc.
—elastic thread or rubber bands (to hold masks in place)

HOW TO MAKE AND USE THEM—

CAUTION: Take care not to frighten young children with a mask. Some young children do not want to wear masks, and they should not be forced to do so. Small eye masks may be a good way to begin. Simply cut eye holes and attach with a rubber band or elastic thread.

1. *Paper Plate Mask.* Make two holes for eyes (begin with small holes and enlarge as needed). Tie elastic thread or rubber band on each side just above the ear. Draw facial features with crayons or felt markers. Encourage children to experiment with faces that are happy, mad, silly, puzzled. Value the faces children create, so that no child's mask is "bad" because of the particular emotion or features portrayed.

2. *Paper Bag Mask.* Use a medium-to-large bag (#10 size is good) and draw on the flat side features and markings, using crayon or felt marker. Roll up a "cuff" at the open end and place bag over the head to decide on placement of eye holes. Then remove the

bag and cut these out, beginning with small holes and checking size and placement as you enlarge.

Part of the top can be cut out for reindeer horns, ears, etc. Pieces of crepe paper, construction paper or pipe cleaner can be glued on as needed for decorations. Use tempera paint mixed with a bit of glue for additional decorations or markings.

3. *Cardboard Boxes.* Children making space men, robots, human computers or other large figures may want to use cardboard boxes. A very large box might be worn over the body and a smaller box on the head.

4. *Papier Mâché Masks.* Masks can be made by shaping papier mâché (see Papier Mâché for recipe) on a flat bowl or mound of clay. Let the strips of paper dry thoroughly before trying to decorate or cut eyes into the mask.

This method will be particularly appropriate if older children want to design more complicated masks or duplicate masks typical of other cultures. A combination of the strip and pulp methods of making papier mâché can be used to design almost any type of mask. Use tempera paints, acrylics or enamels for color and finish. See books on cultures of American Indians, Africa and Asia for specific mask designs.

WHERE TO GET MORE HELP—

Hunt, Kari and Bernice Wells Carlson, *Masks and Mask Makers.* New York and Nashville: Abingdon Press, 1961. 67 pp. $3.50.

metal

WHAT IT IS—

Metals that may be used for learning projects include discarded tin and aluminum cans and lids, aluminum foil plates, TV-type dinner trays and heavy duty broiler foil.

Older children can find many creative uses for metals, which have properties that make them a unique creative medium. In almost every case, children will use tools to work with metal, and this in itself is an important learning opportunity.

WHEN AND WHERE TO USE IT—

Children will need lots of time when they are working with metals, so plan carefully. Working with metal is especially appropriate in craft and camping programs with elementary children.

Children can do projects in any place where they have adequate space to work.

WHY CHILDREN USE IT—

Metals allow children to:
—recycle items to create objects of beauty
—share created objects as gifts
—explore a new dimension of a familiar material
—gain experience in the use of tools.

WHAT CHILDREN NEED—

—tin and aluminum cans in all sizes and shapes (washed and dried)
—foil pans of all sizes and shapes (washed and dried)
—heavy duty broiler foil
—pencils, ball point pens, nails, orange sticks or skewers, sharpened wooden dowel rods (these can be in a variety of thicknesses and are used in tooling)
—ruler or other straight edge
—paints (acrylics, nail polish, enamels)
—newspapers (for padding)
—metal cutters (kitchen scissors with serrated edge and tin shears)
—household or white glue
—used candles and clay

HOW TO DO IT—

Use readily available metal and foils, particularly discarded materials that you can recycle. Notice items in the kitchen, especially cans and pans of many sizes and shapes in which prepared foods are packed. Wash and dry thoroughly. Save all sizes and shapes.

Shaping and Cutting. A cutting tool such as tin shears or heavy scissors can be used to cut the metal into whatever design is desired. Small cuts in the edges can be curled and bent in various ways to simulate a textured surface, like a bird feather.

Tooling. Surface textures can be made by tooling or scoring the metal in various ways. Place the piece of metal on a pad of newspapers and press the point of a tool to make an indentation in the surface. The amount of pressure and the number of times the pressure is applied help determine the kind of pattern. Many variations are possible, such as tooling only the background area in the design so the main design stands out. Encourage children to do lots of experimenting with different tooling instruments (such as pointed sticks, ball point pens, pencils, nails, etc.) so they can begin to see what effect each tool has.

Holes. Punch holes carefully with a sharp tool. Various size nails will make holes of different sizes and shapes when tapped lightly with a hammer. With careful guidance, children can use these tools safely. Older children can also use an awl, which looks like a short ice pick.

Some Metal Projects

1. *Three-dimensional Pictures.* Use aluminum foil pans or trays on a base or background made of wood or heavy cardboard that has been painted or covered with a textured material such as burlap. For a three-dimensional effect in a free-form shape, use scissors to cut and bend the outer edges and sides of the pan into interesting shapes and designs. Use the tooling ideas to add further textures, and make holes in the metal as well. Note how the edges and rims make interesting designs. Use white glue to mount the metal picture onto the background piece and find a place to hang it.

2. *Foil Ornaments.* Fold heavy foil in three or four thicknesses and cut out a shape (see illustration). Do some tooling with all the thicknesses of foil together. You can also make holes in the foil. When complete,

31

separate the foil pieces to create different ornaments. A yarn loop can be glued on the top for hanging. Use as symbols or on an outdoor Christmas tree.

3. *Felt and Foil Ornaments.* Make two identical foil ornaments and glue together with a slightly larger piece of colored felt between them. This ornament is especially effective when many holes are made in the foil so that the color of the felt can show through.

4. *Desk Accessories.* Use a 4- or 5-inch juice can to make a pencil holder for a desk. You may want to paint the inside (and perhaps the outside) of the can with shellac, clear fingernail polish or an enamel. Children will want to choose their own method of decorating the outside of the can. Some possibilities are heavy cord or coarse yarn wrapped around the can and glued in place, enamel or acrylic paint, bits of foil glued on in mosaic style, or self-stick colored vinyl. Cans can also be used to make piggy banks, musical instruments (rhythm instruments), and canisters if they have plastic lids.

5. *Holiday Candle.* Use a large juice can to make a holder for a used candle. Punch holes in interesting patterns all around the sides of the can. Try making the holes in different sizes. Then use a bit of soft clay or some melted wax to set in place in the bottom of the can a partially used candle of any color.

WHERE TO GET MORE HELP—

Sargent, Lucy, *Tin Craft for Christmas.* New York: William Morrow and Co., Inc., 1969. 190 pp. $7.95.

mobiles

WHAT IT IS—

A mobile is a group of objects suspended and balanced so that each piece moves freely in the air. In the

1930s, the sculptor Alexander Calder first suspended and balanced small objects so that they moved in the air to create constantly changing sculpture forms.

Children of all ages enjoy mobiles, and their skill at creating them increases as they grow older.

WHEN AND WHERE TO MAKE THEM—

Children can make mobiles when they want to display in a simple way objects that are light enough to be suspended and balanced in groups. This can be done when an activity is coming to a climax and the children are summarizing or recalling, or when children need to express relationships in a different way.

The delicate balancing required to get a mobile to hang just right may best be done indoors or in a sheltered outdoor spot.

WHY CHILDREN MAKE THEM—

Mobiles allow children to:
—sense and experience the relationship of objects to one another
—observe the effect of air currents on delicately balanced objects *
—assemble in a unique way beautiful objects.

WHAT CHILDREN NEED—

—hangers for the mobile: coat hangers, paper plates, dowel sticks, cardboard paper rolls, stiff wire, tree branch
—thread for hanging objects: sewing thread (especially black), yarns, plastic or nylon fishing line
—for more movement and spinning, buy a packet of fish swivels (at a fishing gear store) and add one to the main supporting thread or line
—scissors, white glue, pliers to twist wire

HOW TO MAKE THEM—

Every mobile needs a central idea or topic—something to unify the various pieces. Typical ideas for children's mobiles are:
nature (things in creation)
seasonal (Easter, Christmas, fall)
symbols (Jesus' life, Old Testament prophets)

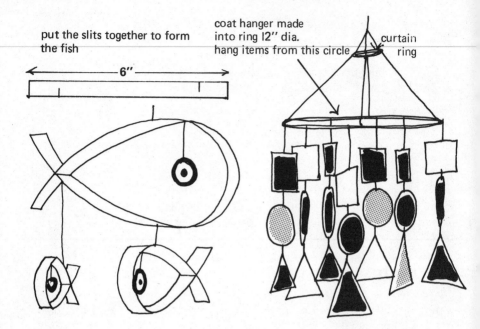

put the slits together to form the fish

6"

coat hanger made into ring 12" dia. hang items from this circle

curtain ring

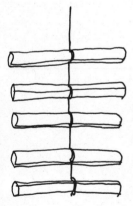

A very simple mobile for younger children involves tying small pictures or pieces of lightweight materials on a coat hanger. These pictures can be torn from paper rather than cut, threaded with colored yarns and tied along the clothes hanger. This type of mobile requires a minimum of balancing. Place a drop of glue at the point where the coat hanger and yarn meet after each item is arranged in its proper place.

Older children will enjoy both making the items to hang on the mobile and trying out their skills in balancing the various parts. Children will want to experiment with many possible designs. A few are sketched above.

A quick word mobile can be made by rolling up single sheets of typing paper and tying them together. You can write an announcement on this, or important words, or special places in map study, or names of special people, etc. Some additional ideas:

1. *Paper Plate Mobile.* Punch holes about 1 inch from the rim of a sturdy paper or plastic-coated plate, spacing them evenly all around the circle. Tie each item on a separate thread and tie to the plate. Topics can be "Things I Like to Do," "The Days of the Week," "The Four Seasons," "Creation in God's World," etc. Hang the mobile by running one thread through a hole in the center of the plate; be sure to knot and glue the thread on the under side so it does not pull through.

2. *Wind Chimes.* Children can make wind chimes by painting or decorating metal can lids, attaching them to strings of various lengths and tying them to a branch of a tree or other large hanger. Space the lids just far enough apart so that as they revolve in the wind they will touch one another.

3. *A Simple Teaching Mobile.* To one strip of cardboard, attach a number of key words relating to the main concept written on the large strip. Attach each word to string or yarn with a paper clip.

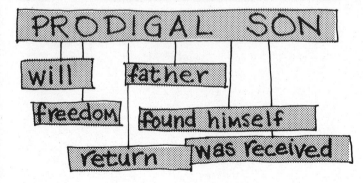

35

models

WHAT THEY ARE—

Models are small-sized three-dimensional replicas. The degree to which the model duplicates the real thing should be flexible. For younger children, cardboard boxes can be houses, boats, farms, cities. And the identity of the object can be changed at will, because it exists in the child's fertile imagination. An older child, on the other hand, may work diligently to re-create an exact likeness of an African village or an Inca temple. Here, the value of the model lies in the exactness of every detail and the struggle with the skills necessary to complete the project.

Many of the cautions observed in the use of dioramas also hold true for making models. See "Some Words of Caution" under Dioramas.

WHEN TO MAKE THEM—

Models are most appropriate when children want to re-create something in a size they can manage themselves. When they're studying church buildings in their community, homes of children around the world or various methods of transportation, they might decide to make some models. When children want to summarize and visualize information in a form they can manipulate themselves, one way to do so is to make models.

WHERE TO MAKE THEM—

Models must be able to be handled and manipulated. For young children this may mean movable and "get-in-able"—perhaps a series of boxes in one corner of a classroom to represent a farm or city, or a similar project in an outdoor play area. Older children will usually make individual models, although several may be combined in a large table-top scene. They will probably work indoors where they have access to materials needed to create a more detailed model.

WHY CHILDREN MAKE THEM—

Models allow children to:

—pull together and synthesize in three-dimensional form certain things they have been studying verbally or through pictures

—reproduce in a size they can manipulate an object or situation distant in time and space

—extend their dexterity and ability to plan and carry out a detailed project

—compare and grow in appreciation of ways different people live, move about, hunt, make their living, etc.

WHAT CHILDREN NEED—

—For box models: boxes of all sizes and varieties (shoe boxes, cereal boxes, oatmeal boxes, milk cartons, hosiery boxes, toothpaste boxes, etc.); material scraps; yarn and pipe cleaners; masking tape, glue; poster or tempera paint; cardboard or plywood for table-top scene.

—For Indian tepee: base of wood or Styrofoam, ten 15-inch-long sticks, fabric or chamois, pins or toothpicks, tempera paints.

—For other homes and transportation: see instructions given for each project.

HOW TO MAKE THEM—

The following are examples of the many kinds of models boys and girls can make:

1. *Box Models for Young Children.* Let young children devise creations of their own by using many kinds of boxes. Show them ways boxes can be attached to each other, but let them decide what to make and how to put it together. Children may make houses, animals, crèche scenes, trains, insects, airplanes or cars or trucks. Young children should be encouraged to be creative. What they do in creating the model and how they will use it are more important than that the model be an exact reproduction of the

original. The boxes can be covered with paint or decorated with material scraps as each child desires.

2. *A Model City or Neighborhood.* Young and middle elementary children may begin to be interested in how things relate to one another in space. Children who show this interest might build a model city or neighborhood with boxes. "Our church and where we live" would help children understand their own church in relationship to where they live in their community. The boxes could be built up and arranged in a table-top scene, or attached more permanently to a piece of cardboard or plywood. The model may be painted to resemble buildings, homes, etc. Here again let the abilities and interests of the child determine the amount of detail.

3. *Models of Indian Homes.* The tepee used by Blackfoot, Sioux, Crow and other tribes can be made by cutting 10 sticks about 15 inches long and gluing them in the familiar tepee pattern to a wood or Styrofoam base. Tie the sticks near the top. Shape a piece of cloth or chamois cut in a semicircular shape with a hole in the center around the sticks. The covering is held together around the poles with pins or toothpicks, and a flapped opening is cut for an entrance.

Designs may then be painted on the tepee to represent animals, mountains, sky, stars, etc.

Simple directions for making tepees and other Indian homes will be found in *Indian Crafts* by Janet and Alex D'Amato (see end of this section).

A Variation—A simple variation on creating homes is to create models of rooms in homes of various cultures. Children could make simple furniture out of cardboard or paper. Rooms could be defined by covering cardboard with different colors of paper or self-stick paper or plastic. These spaces would form the floor space for room arrangements to help children see how persons from India, Japan, Hong Kong, Africa use the space in their homes.

WHERE TO GET MORE HELP—

D'Amato, Janet and Alex, *African Crafts for You to Make*. New York: Julian Messner (div. of Simon & Schuster), 1969. 68 pp. $4.79.

——————————, *Indian Crafts*. New York: Lion Press, Inc., 1968. 65 pp. $3.95.

St. Tamara, *Asian Crafts*. New York: Lion Press, Inc., 1970. 64 pp. $3.95.

montage

WHAT IT IS—

Montage is a collection of individual pictures or photographs arranged to form a composite picture. The emphasis here is on the similar nature of the materials being arranged together and/or the theme they have in common.

WHEN TO DO IT—

Montage may be used when boys and girls wish to use groups of pictures and/or photographs to make a pleasing design or to convey a message. They might be portraying a particular theme or idea; using pictures to get into a new area or to summarize their study; capturing feelings; displaying a particular style of illustration, drawing or photography; or trying to capture in pictures a group of people, who they are and what they are like.

WHERE TO DO IT—

Boys and girls can use montage in almost any classroom setting, as well as outdoors and in situations where children are working on their own. They will need sufficient time to decide what kinds of montage they are trying to create and to select, arrange and paste the pictures.

WHY CHILDREN DO IT—

Montage allows children to:
—evaluate and choose pictures, photographs, advertisements, etc.
—express themselves through pictures rather than through words
—sense the importance of relation, position and arrangement in a group of pictures; sense that their composite picture is more than the sum of the individual pictures it contains
—use pictures to get across a mood or feeling, to express an idea, to explore a theme, to share some information or to impart a message.

WHAT CHILDREN NEED—

—For the montage itself: all kinds of pictures from magazines, catalogs, church story papers, student books, newspapers. Some children may want to draw their own. Colored tissue (in light, pastel or variegated colors) can be pasted over (or over, under and around) the arrangement.
—For the background: sturdy white or plain cardboard. This can be framed (with wood, colored cardboard or construction paper) or made to hang.
—Adhesive: thinned white glue. This can also be used as a fixative when spread over the finished montage. Other fixatives are shellac or plastic spray.
—Permanent black felt marker can be used to outline

certain portions of the montage, i.e. faces, a cluster of figures at the center.

HOW TO DO IT—

Boys and girls need to be clear about their purpose at the beginning. Are they capturing the mood of a color, or are they trying to create a pleasing arrangement? Are they summarizing a unit of study on churches, or are they presenting a collection of pictures of American Indian children?

Make available many, many pictures and let children make selections. Once you have provided materials and helped them know what their purposes are, step back and let the children's imaginations take over.

moSaic

WHAT IT IS—

In mosaic work, a large number of small pieces of material (known as *tesserae)* are attached to a firm surface to make a picture or design. Sometimes these small pieces touch each other; sometimes they are spaced a little apart. Usually, the entire surface is covered and the design is created by large numbers of small pieces filling in sections of the total design. Younger children, however, can use the small pieces simply to outline the shape or object in the picture without filling in all the spaces completely.

WHEN AND WHERE TO DO IT—

Mosaic is most appropriate when a very simple kind of picture or design is desired, since children will not usually be able to incorporate elaborate detail into their designs. This activity is useful when children are experimenting with the size, shape, color and texture of small objects and learning to arrange them in meaningful, interesting or creative patterns.

Mosaics can be made easily in most classroom situations, either formal or informal, indoors or outdoors, by children in groups or working alone. Each child will need time and space to arrange his or her mosaic.

WHY CHILDREN DO IT—

Mosaic allows children to:
—create something beautiful out of common objects
—choose materials in order to accomplish a purpose
—discover new qualities in familiar materials
—have tactile experiences as they arrange and rearrange many objects
—discover mosaic as another way to create a picture or design.

WHAT CHILDREN NEED—

—For the materials to be arranged on the background:
  paper (tiny pieces of colored tissue, newspaper want ads, wrapping paper, etc.)
  postage stamps (either whole or in pieces) for studying countries of the world

pebbles	ceramic tile
shells	glass (small pieces)
seeds	wood, bark
dried beans, peas, corn	cereal
rice	bottle caps
macaroni	buttons
cloth (tiny pieces)	cork pieces
linoleum	nut shells
egg shell (colored and crushed)	foil (tiny pieces)

Note: Care must be used when children are working with small pieces of glass.
—For the background piece:

cardboard	Formica
plywood or boards	china
linoleum	hard plastic

Note: The background piece must be fairly rigid so it will not bend and loosen the mosaic pieces after they have been glued.
—Filling between tesserae: plaster of Paris, ceramic tile grout, clear plastic resin

—Frames: simple cardboard or colored paper mountings; wooden frames.

HOW TO DO IT—

The children will need to decide whether to sketch out their design on the background piece (or on a piece of paper the same size) before they begin gluing, or to create their pattern as they go.

Either method is legitimate. The danger in the former approach, however, is of tracing or reproducing a design slavishly. Boys and girls should make their own designs in very broad shapes, either on the background piece itself (which they may paint first if the background color is important in their design, as it shows through between the tesserae) or on a separate piece of paper.

If they use paper, they simply arrange the tesserae on paper first and then transfer and glue them one by one to the background piece. Another method is to sort the tesserae by sizes and colors, apply glue to small sections of the design one at a time, drop tesserae onto the glued portion and when the glue is dry, shake off excess pieces.

Whichever method the boys and girls use, encourage creativity. If a design is made ahead of time, it should be the child's own and not copied from a book. It can be simple or advanced, but it should be original!

A Variation—Another form of mosaic—more appropriate for older children—requires a plaster base. A slow-drying plaster (see recipe below) is poured into either a temporary or permanent mold, and the tesserae are arranged in the plaster while it is still partially wet. When dry, the mosaic is complete. If a temporary frame was used (a simple wooden frame) this is removed. If the plaster was poured into a permanent frame (such as a pan, a flat tin, or even a picture frame with a backing attached) the mosaic and frame remain together. In each case, embed chicken wire in the plaster to strengthen it, as well as a hook or wire loop for hanging. Most mosaics made by children will probably be the hanging type, although some may make a coaster, tray or trivet.

Recipe—Plaster of Paris (slow-drying)

1 cup water
1 cup plaster of Paris
1 teaspoon vinegar

Add 1 teaspoon vinegar to 1 cup water. Then stir in 1 cup plaster of Paris. Mix with a spoon or stick in a pie pan or heavy plastic bag. The plastic bag makes for easy kneading and easy clean-up.

If you need to speed up the drying process add 1 tablespoon of salt to the liquid plaster.

WHERE TO GET MORE HELP—

Seidelman, James E. and Grace Mintonye, *Creating Mosaics*. New York: Crowell-Collier Press, 1967. 56 pp. $4.95.

MOTION PICTURES (See Films and Filmstrips)

movement

WHAT IT IS—

Movement here refers to the child's interpretation of thoughts and feelings as expressed through the use of the body. Movements may be made in silence or to the accompaniment of singing, percussion instruments, recorded music, or simple rhythmic oral reading or speaking.

We include within the above definition the whole area of pantomime. See the special section on page 47.

A Word About Dance. Creative movement is not dance. Margaret Fisk Taylor explains that dance is an art for exhibition with a set of pre-planned, rigid, structured techniques laid down by a dance expert. For our purposes, technique is unimportant; our goal is to involve each child in genuine natural movement through meaningful participation.

WHEN AND WHERE TO DO IT—

Movement can be used whenever it is appropriate for boys and girls to express their thoughts and feelings through the use of their bodies. This may be done for a few moments or for a longer period of time; along with other activities, or as a special kind of learning experience.

Children can use movement almost anywhere that they have lots of space in which to move freely.

WHY CHILDREN DO IT—

Movement allows children to:
—express what they think and feel about certain ideas in non-verbal ways
—gain increasing control over their own bodies
—use their bodies in acts of meditation
—set the scene for hearing a story, record, or for viewing slides, a filmstrip or a film
—act out important events, especially those the children experience through other media, such as television, to help them understand those events.

WHAT CHILDREN NEED—

—lots of time to experiment
—understanding leaders who can encourage experimentation and give ideas
—record player or tape player (if you want music)

HOW TO DO IT—

Some Beginnings

Movement comes naturally to children. Yet you may find many children who have not been encouraged to discover the world of body movement.

Begin with games that involve such actions as curling up into a ball and walking on tiptoe and being six feet tall. Most often this should be done in a group, without singling out any one person. When a movement is suggested (like "How would you show you were working if you were a clock?"), each person needs to experience it in his or her own way. It's fine for children to share these expressions if they wish, but the particular union of feeling and movement usually cannot be repeated by another person.

Invite the children to give suggestions for body movements out of their own experiences: a clanging fire engine, a bowl full of gelatin, etc. Explore different ways to walk—jerky, smooth, bumpy, stiff, loose, hard, soft, light. Add a character to each walk. Choose a favorite story and walk like each of the characters.

Now spend some time with various movements: swinging, bending, twisting, dodging, shaking, bouncing, pulling, pushing, stretching, etc. What are some ways the body moves? Each action requires a different kind of movement: walking, hopping, jumping, leaping, running, shuffling, creeping, etc. Now try some combinations: walk while shaking off someone or something; run and dodge a passing car; etc. Give the children an opportunity to suggest and try their own combinations.

Combining Movement with a Bible Story

Use creative movement with a Bible story. "Jesus is walking along the dry road to the next town with his disciples and the others who traveled with him." How do you think they would walk? "Now this was not just any day. This was the day that Jesus was going back to Nazareth, his home town, to teach in the synagogue." How do you think they walked on this day? Tired? In good spirits because they were returning home?

Now invite the children to gather around and hear the reading of Mark 6:1-6. After the reading, ask the children to walk as Jesus and his followers may have walked away from Nazareth and to the other villages. (Some ideas: rejected, disappointed, saddened, hopeful that other places will be better.) Allow time for the children to talk about their feelings.

This is a simple example of how children can gain more understanding of the Scriptures by integrating their bodily feelings with their understanding of the story and trying to experience the events by *being* the persons in the narrative.

Some other Bible verses that could be treated in a similar way are:

Lord's Prayer	(Matthew 6:7-15)
The Good Samaritan	(Luke 10:25-37)
Hebrews wandering in the wilderness	(Exodus 15:19-27)
Jesus in the Garden of Gethsemane	(Matthew 26:36-46)

Hymns

Movement can be used as a way of interpreting and understanding hymns. Some examples:

"Now Thank We All Our God"
"This Is My Father's World"
"In Christ There Is No East or West"
"All Creatures of Our God and King"
"For the Beauty of the Earth"
"Rejoice, Rejoice, Rejoice, Give Thanks and Sing"

Pantomime

Pantomime is dramatization through facial expressions and silent bodily movement only. Pantomime is difficult for some children, since sounds and words are so closely associated with most actions.

Pantomime can be fun. Children especially enjoy making it a guessing game: "What am I doing?" The activities portrayed can be familiar ones, such as eating an ice cream cone on a hot day, having a shoelace break while tying a shoe, meeting a good friend who invites you to come along with him, etc.

Another interesting approach is to pantomime the characters in a drawing. The combination of picture study and bodily movement helps both children and adults understand what the artist was trying to show much better than simply looking at the picture.

Additional Exercises in Movement

1. *Mirror Exercise.* Have everyone find a partner; one person takes the part of the person in the mirror. Stand facing each other. Whatever the first person does is immediately repeated by the person in the mirror. Make movements slowly at first and then increase the speed. Then exchange roles.

2. *Passing an Imaginary Object.* Have the group form a circle and give one person an imaginary object.

By your motions give the person some clues about its size and weight. This person will pass it on to the next person, and as it is passed, children can change its size, weight and dimensions. Pass it around until everyone has received it. *Note:* The purpose here is not to guess what the object is each time, but to describe by bodily movement what each object is like, in shape, weight, size, texture, etc.

3. *Join In.* One person gets up and begins to go through the motions of a simple activity. As others think they know what is happening, they join in with a related motion. Or they do something more with the activity. Eventually the whole group is doing motions related to the original activity. Example: getting ready for school, making a garden, cleaning a room, etc.

4. *What Age Am I?* Give clues about the person you are portraying by showing the way that person might walk. Examples: baby, toddler, first grader, school boy, football player, Miss Teenager, mother, father, grandparent, etc.

mural

WHAT IT IS—

A mural is a large area or surface composed of many pictures centering on one theme. Children of all age levels can do murals. Young children can make separate pictures to add to a larger picture. Older children can plan a large picture and divide the responsibilities for producing its various parts—background, scenes, figures, etc.

WHEN AND WHERE TO MAKE IT—

A mural is a good closing activity for a long unit. Murals are also useful when children want to portray something that has many interrelating parts.

You will need room to spread out large pieces of paper on the floor or on a wall. Groups of children working together on specific sections or scenes will need space to work "around" the picture they are creating.

WHY CHILDREN MAKE IT—

Murals allow children to:
—participate in the creation of a large design or picture, which is a welcome relief from their usual smaller-scale work
—work together in developing a project
—share their ideas and drawing skills in telling a story
—express visually the interrelationship of various aspects of a particular subject or idea.

WHAT CHILDREN NEED—

—large pieces of mural paper ("butcher paper" on large rolls is especially useful)
—tempera paint and brushes, or crayon
—chalk for sketching in light lines
—felt markers for outlining and highlighting

HOW TO DO IT—

Begin by helping girls and boys discuss what will be included in their mural. They may need to do some checking and research. The children may want to jot down or list some key ideas, refining the list if necessary. Good subject areas for murals include the culture of a certain country, events in the life of Jesus, seasons of the year, things children do around the world.

Arrange a long piece of mural paper on an unbroken wall or large floor space. Be sure to cover the floor below the mural, especially if you decide to use tempera paint.

Next, divide the space on the paper, marking each section with chalk and identifying its content. Decisions will have to be made about how to divide responsibilities. Try to allow the children to volunteer for the various parts of the work that they would prefer to do. Some children may want to work on the background; others will prefer to do the people.

Note: If the children draw beginning sketches in each section with chalk, they can fill in colors and details after the basic parts are sketched and arranged to suit everyone.

Be sure to allow plenty of time. Some children will work faster than others; some parts of the work take longer than others.

When the entire project is completed, plans should be made to share it with others.

music

WHAT IT IS—

Music is the art of putting sounds together in beautiful and pleasing arrangements by using principles of melody, harmony and rhythm. Words may accompany music.

Some musical activities are dealt with in other sections in this series: Games (see section on "Games With Young Children"), Movement, Records, Rhythm Instruments.

Here we concentrate on several general aspects of using music with children in the church, dealing especially with singing, listening and creating.

Since most adults who work with children in the church do not have special training in music, their use of musical activities must be done simply as part of their total teaching effort. Classroom use of music should come when and where it will best support and correlate with the work already being done.

WHEN TO USE IT—

Children can sing spontaneously when they are alone, and in groups they can frequently use various kinds of musical activities to express their ideas and feelings or to appreciate and respond to the musical expressions of others. Group use of songs or hymns—either written by others or by the children themselves—is especially appropriate when boys and girls want to express or summarize musically their own ideas, thoughts or feelings about what they have learned. The music of people of other cultures is an especially rich heritage, and boys and girls should have opportunity to use and appreciate the music of many peoples.

WHERE TO USE IT—

Activities involving the use of special equipment, like pianos and record players, may be limited to certain places. Generally, however, musical activities are appropriate almost anywhere, in both formal and informal learning situations, indoors and outdoors.

WHY CHILDREN USE IT—

Music allows children to:
—express ideas poetically and musically
—grow in their appreciation of the music of others
—grow in singing skills, both individually and in groups
—improve their listening skills
—increasingly know and appreciate the musical heritage of the church
—gradually improve in their ability to read musical notation.

WHAT CHILDREN NEED—

—opportunities to listen to music appropriate to a particular learning situation
—opportunities to learn and sing many hymns and songs

51

—some simple ideas with which to start in creating their own music

—various kinds of instruments, such as piano, Auto-harp, guitar, melody bells, simple percussion instruments (drums, triangles, clappers, etc.)

—record player (and records), tape recorder (either cassette or reel-to-reel)

—leaders who know children and how they learn as well as have an interest in and understanding of music

HOW TO USE IT—

Our goal in using music with children should be to give them as many different kinds of experiences as possible. Singing is one way to do this.

Group singing is important because everyone participates, and doing it together creates a shared bond that unites the participants. Whether it is a great hymn or a "fun" song, singing fosters a sense of community.

Ideas boys and girls learn through singing are often remembered longer. Singing hymns is one of the most important ways children grow in faith. Theological concepts they pick up in hymns may be the ones they remember longest. Since children usually learn their hymns in a church school class, the singing experiences they have in class are very important for their growing faith.

Using Hymns With Children

Here are some simple suggestions every teacher can use to help boys and girls learn a new hymn:

1. *Know the hymn well.* Then you can concentrate on helping the children learn it.

2. *Vary the ways you introduce hymns.* Several possibilities: (a) learn the text first as a poem, (b) call attention to the tune on some instrument first, (c) help the children learn the rhythmic pattern first, (d) discuss the meaning of the hymn and the story of how it came to be written.

3. *Vary the accompaniment.* Besides the piano, use records, the tape recorder and other instruments, especially those that present the melody clearly.

4. *Add creative movement.* As children become fa-

miliar with the hymn, help them express its meaning with body movement (see Movement).

5. *Use art.* You might (a) display some pictures you have found to help explain the hymn's meaning or (b) have children draw their own pictures to illustrate it. One way to do the latter is to have children express through art the mood suggested by a hymn.

6. *Return to newly learned hymns occasionally.* Keep coming back to a hymn to reinforce the children's familiarity with it.

7. *Select a variety of kinds and styles of hymns, as well as some non-hymnal music.*

8. *Experiment with a hymn to see if it can be dramatized.* See if one of the stanzas or the story of how the hymn came to be written can be acted out by the children. Or act out a situation from the child's own experience that relates to the message of the hymn.

Listening Experiences

Listening experiences must be carefully planned and carried out for maximum effect.

1. Make listening an *active* experience. Give children something to listen *for. Do* something with the experience after it is completed; don't just let it end.

2. Be clear about your own purposes. (a) Do you want children to gain information? Is there something in the content of the song they should get? Help them know how to get it. Is there something about the type or style of music you want children to learn? Give them the necessary background. (b) Do you want children to appreciate a piece of good music? Help them know something about the music first. Give them some guidelines that will help develop appreciation, not boredom. Choose the selection carefully. Don't make it too long! (c) Do you want to create an atmosphere conducive to rest, or worship, or play? Select your music carefully and practice your introduction so that nothing detracts from the atmosphere you are trying to create.

3. Plan technical or mechanical details carefully. If you use a tape recorder or record player, make sure the equipment is in working order. If you are using "live" music, be sure all arrangements are made so

that the musician is ready and prepared at the proper time.

Creating Music

Children need opportunities to create their own musical expressions of various kinds. Since most children are either unskilled or just beginning their formal training in music, their creative efforts, usually improvised, vary widely in results.

Children should be given many opportunities to improvise rhythmic patterns or melodies, to make up poems and set them to improvised tunes, to select various kinds of rhythm instruments to accompany songs, and to make up singing conversations and games on the spur of the moment.

Here are some typical creative musical activities. Children can:

—create new stanzas for a familiar song or hymn, perhaps related to things they are now studying;

—create simple melodies for a familiar poem or a poem that one of the children has written;

—experiment in creating rhythmic patterns by getting everyone to clap out a rhythm that one person has first demonstrated;

—sing conversationally; this can be done just for fun, or to prepare a mood, give directions, provide a transition to a new activity, etc.;

—decide what instruments will best accompany a certain hymn or song; decide how the instruments will be used.

Children can also use art to help them express how music makes them think or feel. If a certain subject lends itself to illustration, try to find a piece of music that relates to the same kind of idea. Play the music and invite the children to draw pictures showing how the music makes them think or feel. Then relate these pictures to the topic they have been studying.

Hints for the Teacher Who Can't Sing

Even if your church curriculum includes flat discs or records, you may want to consider using a cassette tape recorder. (See also Tapes.)

Here are some suggestions:

54

1. Make cassette recordings of all hymns and music for a teaching unit before the unit begins. Then you can play back any music at any time.

2. Recruit a musician in your church to make the tape recording for you. Often someone who can't or won't teach regularly will make a tape recording.

3. Put only one song or hymn on each side of a cassette tape to simplify locating the music you want. Be sure to label each side of each tape.

4. Use as many different musical accompaniments as possible in your tape recordings. Besides piano and organ, can someone use guitar, tone bells or flute?

5. Have older children, or perhaps a youth choir, make recordings for use by the younger children.

Some Questions for Evaluation

We need to evaluate constantly the musical activities we provide for children, since music is such an important part of their training.

Ask yourself these questions:

1. Do our teachers try to provide some type of musical experience in every session?

2. Has our music director or organist helped us develop a workable music philosophy, with some reasonable musical objectives set up for each year?

3. Does our church sponsor—or help sponsor—inservice training for its teachers? Does that training include instruction in music?

4. Do the churches in our area provide resource leaders in church music with children?

nature

WHAT IT IS—

Objects found in nature may be used in creative activities with children. Often such materials provide children with an opportunity to learn about the order and interdependence in our world. Most people respond in special ways to objects from nature—they evoke wonder, appreciation, awe, concern, joy, etc.

WHEN TO USE IT—

The "when" in using objects from nature is often related to the seasons. Dried leaves and grasses may best be found in late summer and autumn in many sections of the country, new leaves and small plants in spring.

The use of nature objects need not be related to a child's specific study, for planting and growing are not necessarily timed to coincide with certain topics. Use nature experiences whenever they can help boys and girls come to a new understanding of themselves and the world about them.

WHERE TO USE IT—

The "where" is also somewhat related to your location. Use those materials that are available where you are, and in a location where children will have easy access to whatever they need. Exercise your ingenuity in using creatively what is available. How many different ways can you use dirt, sand, leaves, limbs, seeds, cones, etc.?

WHY CHILDREN USE IT—

The use of objects from nature allows children to:
—make use of readily available materials
—find patterns and designs that are repeated in various ways in nature
—create something new and beautiful from unrelated nature objects that have their own separate and distinct kind of beauty
—come to appreciate something of the cycles of growth in nature
—develop a sense of the interrelatedness of animals, people and non-living things.

WHAT CHILDREN NEED—

—shells, pebbles, round stones, small stones, sand
—plant materials (leaves, grasses, cones, seeds, limbs or twigs)

56

—transparent adhesive plastic
—colored construction paper
—gummed hook, paper clip and thread, or screw hook
   (for hanging)
—wooden drapery ring, ribbon
—white glue, masking tape, colored plastic tape
—lath wood (for three-dimensional frame)
—plastic clay
—paint (acrylic, tempera)
—felt markers
—felt scraps
—unshelled peanuts
—pipe cleaners
—bird seed, wet sponge, egg shell, potting soil
—peanut butter jar, cotton balls, blotter paper
—seeds (such as lima bean, green bean, melon, corn,
   etc.)
—materials for terrarium

HOW TO USE IT—

A number of nature projects are mentioned in other
sections of this series: see Collage, Construction, Collections, Jewelry, Candles (sand candles), Casting, Pottery, Foods, Prints and Printing, and Rubbings. Following are additional ideas.

1. *Pressing Flowers and Leaves.* Children of almost
any age might gather and press leaves and flowers.
Gather the items when they have the least moisture,
around noon. Separate flower, leaves and stems before pressing. Use one of two methods for pressing:

Method A. Press with no overlapping between
layers of paper toweling. Place under a heavy book or
board.

Method B. Press between the pages of an old book.
Put a weight on top of the book and let the materials
dry for several days.

2. *Using Dried Materials.* To display underneath
plastic, cut pieces of clear adhesive plastic into whatever shape and size you want. Arrange the pressed
pieces into a design and then lay a second piece of
plastic on top, with the sticky sides together.

Or use clear plastic on one side and colored construction paper on the other. On a piece of clear

plastic with the sticky side up, arrange materials so that the "front" of the design will show through the plastic. Then lay a piece of colored construction paper on top for a background.

Be sure to avoid air bubbles as you put the two pieces together, whichever method you use. Seal the edges with colored plastic tape or masking tape.

Such a design can be displayed in a number of ways. A gummed hook can be pasted on a construction paper back for hanging on a wall. A design that has plastic on both sides could be hung in a window so that the light will shine through and reveal the colors in the design. A paper clip tied to thread or string will allow the pressing to revolve in the air as it swings.

3. *Miniature Designs*. Using small, delicate flowers, leaves and grasses, arrange a design that will fit within the inside circle of a wooden drapery ring. Use either method mentioned above and place the plastic or construction paper on the underside of the ring, so that the ring becomes a circular frame for the design. If the design is on a construction paper backing, the items can be glued directly onto the paper without the plastic cover. A small ribbon bow can be added to the eyelet of the drapery ring, which can be either at the top or bottom of the design. The depth of the ring gives a kind of shadow box effect. A small hook could be screwed into the ring back for hanging, or (with the construction paper version) a gummed hook can be pasted on the back.

4. *Three-dimensional Frame*. Use scrap wood (lath wood is best) to create a small frame 2½ x 3 or 3 x 4 inches in size. Depth might be 1½ to 2 inches. Finish the frame with a wipe-on stain or leave natural.

Plan a view of a garden, keeping in mind that your frame is open on both sides. Include high trees and bushes, low bushes and stones, and perhaps tiny animals like birds, rabbits, squirrels, etc.

Push small clumps of plastic-type clay into a bottom corner for a base for a clump of tall trees and bushes. The clay can be covered with a coating of sand or dirt to make it look natural. Use a variety of materials with many textures to achieve the look of a forest of trees. In another area use a smaller lump of clay and insert some short bushes. Glue stones to the bottom to form paths; larger stones can be boulders and rocks. Try to keep all items in perspective and in proper relationship to one another. If animals are desired use paper or clay to create your own.

5. *Nature Creatures.* Use stones or shells to make animals. Owls and turtles can easily be painted onto round stones with acrylic paints. You can make a whole zoo with a variety of rounded stones. Felt bits can be added for eyes.

6. *Peanut Bugs.* Look at a group of unshelled peanuts. Can you see some caterpillars in the shapes? By adding a few stripes and other designs, eyes (using acrylics, tempera or felt markers) and pipecleaner legs, children can create their own peanut creatures. Encourage them to think of other kinds of creatures they can create.

7. *Tiny Gardens*. For a quick-growing garden, plant some bird seed. Young children can use a wet sponge (be sure the sponge is kept wet). Older children can plant seed in half an egg shell filled with potting soil.

8. *Seed Jar*. Make a sprouting jar from a peanut butter jar. In the bottom put several cotton balls. Cut a piece of blotter paper, large enough to fit around the inside of the jar, to hold the seeds near the glass. Place a few of the following seeds between jar and blotter paper: lima bean, green bean, melon, corn or other large seed. Dampen the cotton balls, put the lid on and set the jar in a warm spot. Make a chart to indicate what seems to be happening each day. How long does it take for the seed to sprout? To have two or more leaves? Plant seeds in the soil after the children have studied them.

9. *Tiny Bottle Gardens (Terrariums)*. This is an excellent opportunity for children to watch growth as it takes place.

Here are the things you will need for a terrarium:
—container (jar, bottle, jug, aquarium with plate glass cover; the glass must be clear, and there must be a cover; a large bottle may be planted on its side)
—plants (of various textures: short or dwarf types; look for moss, ivy, ferns, moneywort, partridge berry, hepatica, seeds of citrus, dwarf begonias, coleus, violets)
—charcoal (aquarium type)
—stones or pebbles (washed)
—sterilized potting soil

—spray bottle (for watering)

Clean and sterilize container and lid, using household bleach mixed with water (one part bleach to six parts water). Rinse thoroughly and let dry. Place a layer of large washed gravel in the bottom for drainage. Add ¼ to ½ cup of charcoal to filter the water and keep it sweet. Add soil, making mounds and valleys at least one inch thick over the charcoal. Arrange plants, mosses, rocks, etc. For small-necked bottles, use chopsticks to do the planting.

Add water with a spray bottle. For the first watering, try to get the water level established (about ¼ - ½ cup). Wait 4-12 hours before adding any more water. If too much water gets in, leave the lid off. Water drops will form on the top of the container and will go back down into the soil. Once the water level is established, do not add water for a month or so.

Place the lid on the container and set where it will get some sunlight for a small part of the day. Notice where the moisture is at night. Can you see hair roots growing? Plants can be trimmed with a sharp knife if they get too tall.

Another way of making a top for the container is to use plastic wrap and a rubber band.

WHERE TO GET MORE HELP—

Hoke, John, *Terrariums*. New York: Franklin Watts, Inc., 1972. 90 pp. $3.95.

Pringle, Laurence, *Ecology: Science of Survival*. New York: Macmillan Company, 1971. $4.95.

newspaper

WHAT IT IS—

Newspapers that children create can be freely adapted from the style of daily newspapers with which they are familiar, and will contain some of the same types of features.

WHEN AND WHERE TO USE IT—

Children will use the newspaper format when they want to share ideas with a number of persons. Some groups find the challenge of publishing a weekly or monthly newspaper to be a real motivation to do more writing, interviews and research. For example, an ongoing children's group interested in conservation might decide to produce a newspaper entitled "Recycle News." Such a project would have a great deal of motivation and might be continued for some time.

Other groups find that one edition of a newspaper is sufficient. Such a group might, for example, summarize their unit of study on the Bible lands with a newspaper sharing what they learned. Or the study of another culture could be culminated in this same way, so that information can be shared with others who have not been involved in the study sessions.

This kind of project is most likely to appeal to older elementary children, and adult leaders should not push to continue publications after the children's interest has moved on to other things.

WHY CHILDREN USE IT—

Children may participate in a newspaper project in order to:
—summarize what they have been studying
—share some of their work with others
—influence the interests or understanding of other persons
—experience the leadership role of newspaper staff reporters.

WHAT CHILDREN NEED—

—large sheets of newsprint
—writing paper, pencils
—small and large pointed felt pens for drawing and writing
—plan for reproducing additional copies of the newspaper

HOW TO USE IT—

First, children need to become familiar with local newspapers. Together, look at the various formats. Point out and name the headlines, columns, various departments, etc. Place labels on each of these parts and post the labeled sample on a bulletin board.

Children enjoy writing stories, cartoons, want ads, editorials, letters to the editor, sports stories, etc.

Consider how you will make additional copies. What processes are available: ditto, mimeograph, offset press? The latter process will give the clearest reproduction of the children's own work, including cartoons and pictures. Articles can be typed. With the ditto process the work can be done with pencil, pen or typewriter on special duplicating masters.

Or you may prefer a large newspaper, mocked up on newsprint and posted on the bulletin board.

For additional resources, see Interview, Writing, Story Writing, Photography, Poetry and Puzzles.

over head projection

WHAT IT IS—

We refer here to visuals placed on transparencies and projected on a screen by means of an overhead projector. Commercially prepared visuals are available; however, we emphasize transparencies that children can make and use themselves.

WHEN TO USE IT—

Children can use overhead projection when they have a report to make, when they want to share a chart, map or diagram, when they want a group to be able to read words to a song or poem, or when they want to project a set of instructions for others to follow.

WHERE TO USE IT—

Children will use overhead projection in classroom or meeting room situations where the necessary equipment is available. Since overhead projection does not require a darkened room, almost any room will do.

WHY CHILDREN USE IT—

Overhead projection allows children to:
—share information simultaneously with a group of almost any size
—prepare transparencies by hand
—use projection equipment successfully
—experiment with different methods and materials in making transparencies.

WHAT CHILDREN NEED—

—an overhead projector
—a projection screen
—materials to make their own transparencies:
  —large plastic bags, transparent plastic or acetate sheeting, heavy duty freezer wrapping plastic
  —colored plastic tape
  —water-soluble overhead projection pens (check quality on these, as some brands are better than others)
  —large pieces of cardboard, poster board or manila file folders (for making frames)
  —damp cloth

HOW TO DO IT—

The overhead projector sits on a flat surface about 6 to 8 feet in front of a projection screen. A transparency is laid on a glass surface on the top of the projector and the image projected on the screen. By means of light and mirrors, the image on a transparency approximately 8½ x 11 inches will be projected in an enlarged size on the screen.

Any words, pictures, drawings, diagrams, etc. that can be made into a transparency can be projected. Often, through the use of certain kinds of overhead projection pens, the image can be projected in colors.

Making Simple Transparencies. Large plastic bags,

pieces of transparent plastic or acetate sheeting, or heavy duty plastic freezer wrapping can be used. Cut the plastic to an 8½ x 11-inch size. To use without a frame, place it carefully on the glass surface, making certain any places where it does not lie flat are smoothed out. Plastic can be framed with colored plastic tape to give it some strength and keep it in shape. A frame can also be cut from a large piece of cardboard, poster board, or from one half of a manila file folder, and the transparency taped to it. Once the plastic is in place on the projector, children will write on it with a good water-soluble overhead projection pen just as they would on any other kind of plastic or paper. The transparency can be wiped clean at any time with a damp cloth and reused.

Children will find many uses for overhead transparencies. Words of songs can be written on them for use in worship, as can words of a litany, prayer, response or choral reading. Committees can use transparencies to outline their findings, key words, maps, charts, lists, names of places or persons, etc.

painting

WHAT IT IS—

Painting is the application of color to surfaces with a brush or a brush substitute. See also Prints and Printing, Crayons, Sensory Experiences (soap painting).

WHEN AND WHERE TO DO IT—

Children can use painting techniques any time they want to create a picture or design. Some painting procedures can be done in a single classroom period while others cannot. Painting experiences can begin with young children even before they have full command of spoken language and can continue throughout life as a means of non-verbal expression.

Children can paint almost any place, indoors or outdoors, using the floor, wall space, a table top, a painting easel, or any flat space.

WHY CHILDREN DO IT—

Painting allows children to:
—create a picture or design, using color
—express a feeling or idea non-verbally
—create an environment (as in painted background scenes, murals, etc.)
—decorate items they have created
—make a non-verbal response to a story, music, a trip, etc.
—experiment with color, shape, design and texture
—learn about the properties of various types of paints and painting surfaces.

WHAT CHILDREN NEED—

—various types of paint:
  (*Note:* Choose the type of paint to suit the children's purposes)
  —tempera:
    —sold in many rich colors in powdered or liquid form, in school supply or art supply stores (Use liquid starch and/or wheat paste with powdered form)
    —most often used on small items, paper, self-hardening clay, etc.
    —can be mixed with other media (starch to make finger paint, coloring for clay, dyeing for pipe cleaners, etc.)
    —fast drying but not waterproof
  —acrylics:
    —water soluble but permanent when dry; will stick to unusual surfaces like rocks, metals and coarse paper
    —can be built up like oil paints to provide texture
    —comes in tubes in many colors
    —dries quickly
  —water colors:
    —come in small pans of dry color or premixed in tubes

—give a delicate coloring
—usually used for background washes and fine details
—best for older elementary children who can have satisfying experiences with smaller detail
—outdoor paints:
  —latex and oil base house paints and acrylic enamels
  —for use with cardboard boxes, wood and metal
  —necessary when large surfaces are to be painted
  —important for outdoor items, such as playground equipment, fences, walls, etc.
  —use rust preventative paint in colors when painting on metal
  —use acrylic enamel on cardboard storage boxes to strengthen the cardboard
—chalk:
  —use a soft chalk in deep rich colors, rather than a hard chalkboard chalk, as a paint substitute
—various painting surfaces:
  —paper:
    —all kinds from newsprint to poster board, mural paper and shelf paper
    —large surfaces are best for younger children and for "giant" paintings
    —use finger paint paper or shiny shelf paper for finger painting
  —cardboard:
    —corrugated paper boxes, heavy cardboard, fabric bolts
  —wood:
    —all types of wood scraps
    —end cuts of wood logs from a sawmill with bark on one side
—brushes and brush substitutes:
  —brushes:
    —collect a wide variety with soft bristles
    —use thin ones for water colors and small details when using tempera
    —young children need ½-inch brushes
    —1½ or 2-inch brushes for outdoor paints and large surfaces

—brush substitutes:
  —1-inch squares of sponge and clip-type clothes
    pins for sponge painting
  —pieces of string in various thicknesses and tex-
    tures
  —toothbrush, screen, ruler for spatter painting
    (see Stenciling)
  —paste sticks, spools for string painting
—miscellaneous:
  —holders for paint: jars, muffin tins, orange juice
    cans, foil pans, etc. (Note: Paints should be stored
    in sealed containers to keep them from drying
    out.)
  —paint shirts (used men's shirts turned backward
    and with sleeves cut short) or smocks. (Note: For
    younger children, line the shirt back with heavy
    plastic, so that paint will not soak through onto
    their clothes.)
  —lots of newspapers or plastic sheeting to cover the
    floor in the painting area.
  —A place to dry finished paintings (clothes line and
    clothes pins, laundry drying rack, floor space away
    from feet).

HOW TO DO IT—

Using Tempera Paint

Tempera paint, a basic painting medium for children of all ages, can be used in many ways. Liquid
tempera is now available and is used as it comes in
the container. Dry tempera powder must be mixed
with liquid to a creamy consistency. One way to do
this is to add powdered tempera directly to liquid
starch. Or make a paste, using ¼ cup water and 1
teaspoon dry wheat paste (wallpaper paste). Then add
¼ cup liquid starch to achieve the proper consistency.
Finally, add powdered tempera for color. For easy
clean-ups, add one tablespoon of granulated detergent.

Brush painting with tempera is a basic painting experience. For young children, use a painting easel, the
floor or a table top and large (18 x 24-inch) pieces
of plain newsprint or drawing paper. Older children

will use brushes and tempera for various purposes: drawing pictures, making murals, decorating various items, etc.

In addition to flat surfaces, try other surfaces for brush painting. End cuts of logs can be obtained from a sawmill. These can then be painted (either on the bark side or on the one flat side) by young children as wall decorations. Constructions, puppets, clay items, wooden creations can also be painted with tempera by older children.

Most important, let children at all ages have lots of freedom to explore with tempera and brush. Some additional tempera experiences are:

1. *Sponge Painting.* Use clip-type clothes pins to grip a small square of sponge. Dip the sponge in tempera made a bit thicker than usual and then make shapes and designs by pressing the sponge onto paper, wood, cardboard, etc.

2. *Blot Painting.* Fold a piece of construction paper or painting paper in half. Have children place some dots of paint (one or more colors) on one half of the paper and then fold it again, pressing down. Open the paper again to see the total painting. This is a good intergenerational activity, since no blot painter ever knows what kind of picture will appear.

3. *String Painting.* Tie pieces of string of different thicknesses and textures onto individual spools or paste sticks. Place the tempera paint in shallow containers, such as foil pans. Wet the string in tempera and pull it over the paper for interesting effects. Or use the folding technique: the paper is folded in half and the wet string placed on one half; then the paper is pressed back down over the wet string. While the paper is pressed down, the string is removed, making an interesting pattern on both halves of the paper. String painting designs make good booklet covers or designs for box lids.

4. *Blown Painting.* A fairly runny tempera mixture is needed here, as well as paper and drinking straws. Children should drop some dots of paint on their papers and then blow at the paint through the drinking straws. The paint will run in whatever direction the

child is blowing. Turn the paper to change directions. Try several colors.

5. *Spatter Painting*. (See Stenciling.)

6. *Finger Painting*. Finger painting requires a thicker paint, and this can be made (see recipes, this section) or purchased. Use it on wet shelf paper, finger paint paper, or on smooth surfaces like trays, cookie sheets, or Formica table tops. Dampen the paper with a sponge and place several tablespoons of paint onto the paper. Children then begin to move the paint around with fingers, hands and sometimes even arms! Finger painting is a movement experience as much as a painting experience, especially with younger children. Older children can begin to add a second color and create recognizable shapes, sometimes even telling a story. Finger paintings make excellent backgrounds for dioramas, displays and water pictures. Finger painting is also an excellent way of helping children express feelings. Combine finger painting with music and see how they respond to the rhythm as they paint. To make a print from a finger painting, see Prints and Printing.

Non-cooked Finger Paint

liquid starch
dry tempera

Place liquid starch (about two tablespoonsful) on a piece of dampened shiny-surfaced paper. Dust dry tempera into starch. Work the color into the starch and then make designs with both hands. A very quick method with young children.

Cooked Finger Paint

1 cup cornstarch (or laundry starch)	Powdered tempera or food coloring
1 cup Ivory Flakes	1 quart water
½ cup salt	1 teaspoon glycerine

Mix cornstarch with enough cold water to make a thin, smooth paste. Add soap flakes (not granulated) and salt. Put into a double boiler and add one quart of water. Cook until thick, adding more water as necessary. Beat with a rotary egg beater until smooth. Add glycerine to make paint pliable and to prevent cracking when dry. The salt serves as a preservative.

Optional: Add a few drops of oil of wintergreen or cloves for odor. Place cooked paint in small jars with lids. Then add powdered tempera or food coloring for color. Mix and seal.

7. *Other Variations.* To tempera paints, add salt, sand or dirt for a rough texture. Add white glue, library paste or evaporated milk for a shiny texture when dry. Try different brush substitutes: cotton balls, fork tynes, cookie cutters, paste sticks, etc.

Using Acrylics

Acrylic paints come in tubes and should be squeezed out in very small amounts, since they dry so quickly. Use nylon bristle brushes in ¼ to ½-inch size. Use acrylic paint on Formica samples, wood, Masonite, Styrofoam cartons, egg cartons, x-ray paper, stones and many other unusual surfaces. With young children, foam egg cartons may be used as palettes.

Using Chalk for Painting

Select a soft colored chalk in very bright colors, and use various textures of paper. Also try various treatments, such as: (1) construction paper dampened with a sponge, (2) chalk dipped in liquid starch and used on dry paper, (3) paper dampened with a solution of water and powdered milk or (4) a solution of buttermilk and water.

Since colored chalk painting is best for achieving large sweeps of bright colors, do not encourage children to try for fine details. These can be added later.

A completed chalk painting can be made permanent when dry by spraying with a commercial fixative or with a mixture of one part shellac and two or three parts alcohol sprayed with an insect spray gun.

Water Colors

Older children can control the amount of water used in the dry water color pans and enjoy the finer detail in paintings done with small artist brushes. These paints are especially appropriate for delicate Oriental-type drawings and background washes in pictures. For many children this paint is less satisfying than tempera or acrylics—we suggest the tempera for more general use.

Outdoor Paints

When large surfaces need to be covered and water-proofed, use house paints. Choose them for the particular job: latex base, oil base, enamels, rust preventative for metal.

To strengthen cardboard storage boxes, coat them with enamel. Outdoor items like playground equipment should be painted with enamels. Children particularly enjoy painting their playground storage boxes, etc.

Frequently, backgrounds need to be painted before you build a construction, lay a mosaic, begin a decoupage, etc. Choose the paint that best suits the particular job you are doing.

Oil Paints

Many children find oil paints unsatisfactory. They are more difficult to use, and require considerable skill. Thus, we do not recommend oils with children. Use acrylics when a build-up of paint is needed.

WHERE TO GET MORE HELP—

Wright, Kathryn S., *Let the Children Paint: Art in Religious Education.* New York: The Seabury Press, 1966. 168 pp. $4.50.

PANTOMIME (see Movement)

paper

WHAT IT IS—

Paper comes in many colors, textures and thicknesses. It can be worked into many shapes, folded, scored, cut, torn, glued or stapled to make many kinds of objects. (See also Collage, Construction and Display.)

WHEN AND WHERE TO USE IT—

Children use paper any time and almost anywhere. Some paper projects will take very little time; others will require more time. Some will require a flat working surface and plenty of space; others can be done on the ground, in the lap, on the floor, indoors, outdoors, etc.

WHY CHILDREN USE IT—

Paper allows children to:
—use a readily available material that comes in a wide range of types, colors and textures
—learn to manipulate various types and textures of paper
—create objects that can be repeated and duplicated
—create three-dimensional items
—be creative without using many special skills or pieces of equipment.

WHAT CHILDREN NEED—

—paper: Collect as many types, colors, thicknesses, textures and stiffnesses as possible. Plan ahead as you collect, thinking of which kinds will best accomplish your purposes. (Keep a box of paper scraps and add to it constantly.)
—glue: White protein-type glue usually works best, and it dries to be almost invisible. Buy it by the quart (or larger) container and pour into smaller glue bottles, lids or small aluminum pans so that it can be applied with a glue brush or small stick. White glue can be mixed with liquid tempera paint for coloring and diluted with water for gluing and for a finishing treatment.
Rubber cement cleans up easily if too much is applied. A virtually permanent bond is achieved by applying rubber cement to both surfaces and allowing the glue to dry slightly and become tacky before joining them.
—scissors: Children should use good quality scissors that work freely and are easy on their fingers. These can be sharpened on electric knife sharpeners that are marked for scissors sharpening. Consider pur-

chasing heavier household scissors for paper projects, since they are efficient and do a good job of cutting. For younger children, round-ended scissors are desirable. Some very delicate cutting operations will require small scissors.

HOW TO USE IT—

Beginning Activities with Paper

Children should first experiment with some basic paper activities. Eleven exercises are suggested here for this purpose. Exercises 1 through 9 can all be done individually or in some combination, while the last two are to be done individually. If working in groups, children should share results after each exercise. Have available a variety of types of paper, including newsprint, typing paper, construction paper, oak tag and poster board.

1. Cut a lightweight sheet of paper into two pieces of equal size. Ask children to work the paper into various shapes without cutting it. Have them demonstrate two ways, using both pieces of paper. Possible ways of working with the paper include bending, accordion folds, crushing, folding, curling, spiraling, etc. The children can hold their shapes in their hands if they will not stay in place. One child made an ice cream cone with her two pieces of paper.

2. Give each child a half sheet of medium weight paper and paper clips, straight pins or a stapler. Ask them, without using scissors, to make a shape that needs to be held together.

3. Take four or more squares of paper (using several textures) and a pair of scissors. Make each piece into a different shape by cutting part of it away.

4. Give each child two sheets of paper and ask them to develop a way for each piece to stand up.

5. Use the stand-up pieces from exercise 4 and ask children to use scissors or their fingers to make parts of those pieces stick out or be raised for an added three-dimensional effect. Some can be folded, cut, pushed, torn. Accordion folds can be added. Sections can be partially cut out and folded.

6. Pull small pieces of paper quickly but firmly over

the sharp edge of scissors or a ruler, across the edge of a table, or across a pencil or pen to curl paper. Experiment with different weights of paper, and decide which method worked best for each.

7. To practice folding on a curve, children need a fairly heavy piece of paper and scissors or a pen. Make a score line by passing a scissors blade or ball point pen over the paper in a curved line. Then fold the paper along this score line by applying pressure with fingers. Additional folds can be made on the same paper, especially with folds alternating accordion-style and curving out from one point so that the one piece of paper forms a shape like a bird wing, fish fin or graceful leaf.

8. Ask children to attach one piece of paper to another without using paper clips, paste, staples, pins or tape. See if they can discover slits, interlocking slits, tabs, folding or twisting methods to use here.

9. Ask children to use as many techniques in exercises 1 through 8 as they can to create a three-dimensional picture or design. Suggest that they use one large sheet of paper and a variety of smaller ones. Use a minimum of pins, staples, clips.

10. Experiment with cuts:

A. Give each person a 3-inch circle of colored paper and a pair of scissors. Ask them to make as many straight cuts completely through this circle as they wish, and form a design by gluing the cut pieces onto white or a contrasting color of paper.

B. Give each person a 3-inch triangle of colored paper and ask them to make curved cuts through the triangle. Arrange and glue onto a paper background.

C. Give each person a 3-inch square or rectangle of colored paper; ask them to cut long narrow pieces and make a design.

11. Give each person a piece of construction paper and ask them to tear (without scissors) a design or shape or something they like or something that is important to them. This makes an excellent get-acquainted activity, and can also be used to make name tags—place a loop of masking tape on the back of the shape.

Tissue Paper

Colored tissue paper comes in a glorious rainbow of colors. Encourage children to experiment with tissue. Here are some suggestions:

1. *Three-dimensional Tissue Designs and Shapes.* Cut out of heavy construction paper any large design or shape for a base. Then cut 1-inch squares of tissue in various colors. Place the tissue square over the blunt end of a pen or pencil and fold to resemble a miniature cupcake paper. The flat center section can then be glued to the construction paper base. Glue many tissue pieces close together, covering the entire surface (or some part of the surface). The small pieces of tissue will stand out away from the base, creating exciting and colorful designs. Flowers and butterflies are especially beautiful when done this way. (See Kites for a tissue kite for young children to make.)

2. *Covering Other Surfaces With Tissue.* Small pieces of colored tissue can be glued over many surfaces in mosaic style; by overlapping the tissue you can create additional color combinations. This can be done with cardboard boxes, jars, lamp shades, desk sets, etc. A large piece of poster board can be covered and framed with cloth tape or a wooden frame. (*Note:* Any surface that has a design printed on it, like a box with a label, will need a coat of latex or enamel paint so that the tissue is glued onto a plain colored surface.) First, brush the entire surface with a coat of diluted white glue (three parts glue to one part water). Then

apply the tissue pieces one at a time. When finished, add an additional coat of diluted white glue. Let dry thoroughly and trim away any excess tissue around the top of a jar or box. (See Glass for simulated stained glass or transparencies using tissue paper.)

3. *Tissue Flowers.* You will need colored tissue or facial tissue in various colors, 24-gauge wire, and some florist or green cloth tape. Cut tissue into 8x10-inch pieces. Fold accordion style, with folds about ½ inch in width. Bend the tissue in the middle and place a length of wire over the fold. Twist the wire to secure the tissue, and then bend both sides of the folded tissue up together. Twist wire again around the tissue, forming the base of the flower.

Now trim tissue so that the flower petals are uneven and shaped. Wind green florist tape or cloth tape around the base of the flower and down the wire. Leaves can be added if desired.

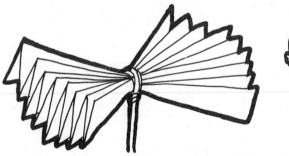

Crepe Paper

Crepe paper will stretch, can be shaped and sewn, and is available in a great variety of colors. Encourage children to experiment with a piece. Which direction has the most stretch? What can be done with the edges? How far can it be pulled before it breaks?

1. *Simple Butterfly.* Cut three 5x3-inch pieces of crepe paper in different colors. Place the three pieces on top of one another in a stack. Pinch the paper together at the center of the 5-inch side, leaving 2½ inches on each side for the wings. Squeeze it together until the center is very narrow. Then fold a pipe cleaner around the fold, with the two ends at the top. Twist

the ends together once and curve them for feelers. (*Note:* The pipe cleaners can be dyed black and dried prior to this project.) These can be used for Easter symbols of the Resurrection, as well as springtime additions to flower arrangements, mobiles, etc. Attach a long wire to the body so you can add the butterfly to a potted plant.

2. *Flowers.* Individual petals or a long strip of petals can be cut out and wrapped around a center. Keep these as simple as possible, since many flowers are more difficult than children are interested in making.

curl petals over scissors and bend out, add a flower center.

Lifelike flowers can be made from craft paper, a form of crepe paper that has two colors, one on each side. Booklets on making flowers are often sold where crepe paper is sold.

3. *Clothing.* Crepe paper can be handled much like cloth and is often used for costumes such as hats, skirts and tunics. Cut as you would fabric and sew on a sewing machine. Reinforce the seam with bias tape if you wish.

4. *A Surprise Ball.* Cut strips of crepe paper about 2 x 36 inches. Choose several small gift items, such as a small top, a ring or a pretty pebble or tiny shell. Start with one piece of crepe paper and the largest gift item. Begin to wrap the item, covering all of it as you wrap around. Stretch the paper as you need to in order to make the covering as round as possible. Add other small surprises and cover each completely. As you add each strip of paper, tuck in the end and apply a tiny bit of glue. On the last piece, glue the edge of the strip to keep it rolled up. These make excellent party surprises and hospital gifts for children.

Metallic Papers

As you collect papers, be sure to collect foil and gift wrappings, as well as the kitchen type of aluminum foil. Interesting effects are achieved by rolling the foil in your hand and then spreading it out beneath tissue for a crinkled or aged effect.

1. *Foil and Tissue Ornaments.* Ornaments can be made by cutting two identical shapes out of heavy paper or cardboard. Cut open spaces in the middle. Place foil between two sheets of tissue and glue the tissue-foil-tissue section between the two identical ornament shapes. Or cut away tissue here and there, letting the foil show through so that it reflects the light.

2. *Foil Paper Finishes.* Some metallic paper is heavy enough so that dull instruments—your fingernail or a pencil eraser—can be used on it to do "tooling" like that done on metal. Do this after the foil is in place on whatever surface you want to appear tooled. Or glue heavy cord in a design on a surface, such as the lid of a box. When the glue is dry, cover the lid with foil, pushing it down around the glued cord for a three-dimensional effect. Glue the foil paper in place at the edges.

Brown Wrapping Paper or Grocery Bags

Use large grocery bags for "stuffies." Make an outline of an animal or shape and cut two the same size. Use glue or staples to fasten the two pieces together, leaving a hole large enough to fill the stuffie with light-weight paper such as newsprint. Trim around the edges after the glue is dry or the stapling finished. On the outside add additional details with felt markers, liquid tempera paint mixed with white glue or glued-on paper pieces. The stuffie can be suspended from a string.

(See also Puppets and Masks.)

Rice Paper

Rice paper is found in art stores and has the Oriental beauty of texture and opaque quality. Use it when a delicate touch is needed.

Make simulated rice paper by covering a piece of kitchen wax paper with white glue. On the wet glue place small pieces of natural items like flower petals, small colored leaves, or bits of colored string, confetti, glitter, etc. Over this lay one layer of white facial tissue (separate a single tissue, which usually has two layers), pressing down with dampened fingers. Let the glue dry thoroughly. This process can be used to make interesting window coverings, decorations for stationery, room dividers, etc.

Block Printing Paper

This is purchased at an art store and has a soft finish with a very attractive texture. It can be used in place of rice paper or for making block prints, and comes in sheets of assorted sizes.

Corrugated Paper

This can be purchased in many colors for attractive bulletin board displays. It also adds a special texture for regular craft work.

Additional Suggestions for Using Paper

1. Paper Folding. This is an art in itself that the Japanese call "origami." An exciting activity for older elementary children, it requires specific folding skills and careful attention to instructions. Look for books on origami where origami paper is sold.

One simple but useful paper folding technique is the Jacob's ladder or paper spring. Cut two pieces of

paper the same length and width. A half-inch width is a workable size. Glue the two ends together as shown. Starting with the bottom piece, fold over first one piece and then the other until you reach the ends of the strips. Then glue the ends together. These expandable springs can be used for legs, arms, handles of baskets, etc.

2. *Paper Cutting*. This skill has been elevated to an art by the Chinese.

Paper snowflakes make an easy paper cutting project. Children will need to be able to fold light paper and then cut small pieces out of the folded paper. Scientists tell us that snowflakes are each different and that they are hexagonal (six-sided). Children will find four-sided snowflakes easiest to make.

Fold a square piece of paper into quarters. Then fold the quartered section diagonally with a third fold. Now cut into both folded sides and also the outside edge with many small cuts, leaving a number of spaces along the folded edges to hold the paper together.

3. *Paper Sculpture*. Paper sculpture involves creating three-dimensional effects through cutting, folding, scoring and curling. The real skill comes in knowing what the paper will do and in being able to experiment with heavy paper and simple tools.

Use heavy drawing paper, 80 lb. construction paper, art paper or craft paper. Rulers, pencils, compasses or other round objects and sharp scissors will be needed. Glue, tape, staples, pins, paper fasteners, or tabs and slits can be used to hold paper shapes together.

One basic experience is making cylinders out of heavy paper. Use the curling technique (see exercise 6) with heavy paper to make some tight cylinders and some loose ones. This involves curling in just one direction.

Another basic experience involves curling in two directions. Using a narrow strip, pull one half of the paper in one direction, curling it up into one circle. Turn it over and pull the other half in the opposite direction. When you have both circles curled, you should have a figure eight shape. Make some that are tight and some that are loose.

Another basic sculpture experience is making cones. Give each child two circles. Make one cut to the center of the circle and, by overlapping and stapling or gluing, make a large cone. What might this shape suggest? Cut the second circle into halves and cut one half in half again. Make cones out of these three pieces. What can these be used for? Arms, legs, hats, flowers, bases for things, trees, etc. What size cones will larger circles make? Try many sizes.

Scoring is very important in paper sculpture. Practice again the scoring techniques in exercise 7, especially the series of folds in opposite directions, or the accordion fold. See how many different shapes you can give to a single large piece of paper.

Another variation on curling is to pull different sections of a piece of paper so that the curving gives the effect of motion, like a flag waving in the breeze. Try this with a piece of paper 2 x 4 inches, pulling it across a ruler at several points. Pull one end into one curve and the other end into a second curve. Use drinking straws or a spiral of paper for a flagpole. Paper pulled in this way can be used for horse tails, hair in the wind, palm trees and other objects where the illusion of motion is desired. Some borders can also be edged with this technique for interesting effects.

flower center

Score and bend
each petal,
add center.

Score on
broken line

tab

Use these beginning techniques to create human figures, animals and nature objects. Also, many symbols can be made of paper and given a three-dimensional treatment. See the illustration of the shield and the budded cross.

Letters of the alphabet can be scored and bent into interesting effects for bulletin boards, displays and decorations. Have children do their own initials in paper sculpture.

4. *Celebration Chains*. Cut from paper a large number of identical shapes, such as hearts, flowers, trees, etc. Place a long piece of heavy thread or ribbon flat on a table. Glue two designs together, with the thread placed between. Space the designs every 10-12 inches along the thread. Seasonal decorations or symbols of a particular culture can be displayed in this way.

papier mâché

WHAT IT IS—

Papier mâché is a material made of paper and paste, that can be modeled into new shapes or used to cover objects.

WHEN TO USE IT—

Children use papier mâché to create three-dimensional objects in a fairly permanent form. It is a good medium to use when children are trying to reproduce their own versions of something, such as animals, masks, or decorations from another culture.

Children should use papier mâché when they have adequate time to complete the process. The actual shaping process is done fairly quickly, but drying time is necessary before the object can be sanded, painted and finished.

WHERE TO USE IT—

Children will need plenty of work space. A table top covered with newspapers is a necessity, as are water and a place for objects to dry.

WHY CHILDREN USE IT—

Papier mâché allows children to:
—make decorations from a culture they are studying
—make inexpensive figures that look like sculpture
—grow in their ability to express proportion, shape and size
—create items for household use
—learn to create figures built over wire, cardboard tubes, or balloons

WHAT CHILDREN NEED—

—a large supply of newspaper
—clean paper for final layers (paper toweling, paper napkins, facial tissues)

—glues (wallpaper wheat paste, white glue, laundry starch, polymer medium, various commercial products)

—materials for armatures (balloons, chicken wire, coat hanger or other heavy wire, cardboard tubes, paper bags—these are the forms being covered)

—instant papier mâché (a commercial product to which water is added to make a pulp type of papier mâché)

—forms to use as bases for the strip method (boxes, bowls, dishes, etc.)

—petroleum jelly, plastic wrap

—paints (tempera, enamel, acrylics)

HOW TO DO IT—

There are two basic ways of working with papier mâché: the strip method and the pulp method. Each is described here, although the strip method is recommended for children.

Strip Method

1. On Flat or Curved Surfaces. A simple way of using the strip method is over flat or curved surfaces, such as plates, dishes or bowls. Use this approach with novices and with kindergartners and younger elementary children.

Cut or tear strips of newspaper about 7 x 1 inches. With younger children, liquid laundry starch can be used as a glue, while those with more experience can use wheat paste diluted with either white glue or polymer medium (which dry more quickly and are waterproof).

Let's use as an example a simple bowl. Cover the bowl generously with petroleum jelly and a layer of plastic wrap, so that it can be easily removed after the papier mâché is dry. The children should dip the paper strips in glue and lay them criss-cross over the outside of the bowl. Continue until the entire bowl has been covered with ten or more layers of newspaper strips. Help children learn how to push out all air bubbles as they place the strips. This will assure a tighter bond. Let the papier mâché dry. Then remove the bowl and trim the edges of the papier mâché bowl for an even surface. The bowl can be coated with tempera paint mixed with white glue or polymer medium, or with enamel paint.

This method can be used also for ash trays, candy dishes, snack trays, etc.

Variations include bracelets and napkin rings, but here the basic shape on which the papier mâché is placed will not be removed. Use a piece of a cardboard mailing tube or a cardboard roll from masking tape. Place the layers of papier mâché strips around all sides of the armature, let dry, and then paint with acrylic paints for bright coloring. Napkin rings can be made with smaller cardboard tubing.

You can also use all kinds of shapes for holders or containers—pencil holders (tin cans), flower holders (jars), notepaper holders (cardboard boxes), and facial tissue holders (cardboard boxes).

2. *On Three-Dimensional Shapes.* Another way to use the strip method is to cover some three-dimensional object completely. Inflated balloons, rolled-up newspaper, paper bags stuffed with newspaper or a figure made of wire can be covered in this manner. The form to be covered is the armature.

First, make the armature. Often these provide the basic shape only, since the papier mâché can be used to build up the details.

Let's use the elephant (see illustration) as an example. Tear paper into long narrow strips and dip into a creamy paste (white glue slightly diluted or wheat paste). Begin by adding strips lengthwise along the back, starting at the end of the tail and moving up the back, over the head and down the trunk. Then add strips in the other direction. Alternate directions as you add, and be sure to move back and forth so that no one area gets too much of a build-up. Shape the strips into place as you go. Overlap and criss-cross the strips. In areas that need to be built up before being covered with strips—ears, horns, nose, mouth, tails, some clothing, etc.—use small wads of paper or cotton.

When the animal has reached its final shape, you may want to add one last layer of "clean" paper (paper

towel, napkins or facial tissue). If you plan to paint the entire object, this may not be necessary. You may also glue the last layer with white glue or polymer medium. When the object is thoroughly dry, you can sand and paint with tempera or enamel.

3. *Pinatas.* Make an animal or other figure around a large balloon or paper bag, using the strip method. Between two layers, tie some string around the middle of the figure, and then continue adding strips. This will allow you to hang up the pinata when it is finished. Do not use too many layers, because the pinata should break when hit with a stick. When dry, cut a large slit in the top, and fill with candies and trinkets.

Children take turns being blindfolded. Then, after being spun around, they try to break the pinata open. When that happens, all scurry for goodies.

4. *Animal Shapes.* Tape paper tubes together to make the armature and build up until you get the final shape of the animal you are creating. Add details of ears, tail, etc. near the end.

5. *Eggs.* Make small egg shapes over balloons, using very thin strips of paper, and decorate; an excellent opportunity for children to work with oval shapes.

6. *Nativity Figures.* Use various sizes of cardboard or

Styrofoam cones plus Styrofoam balls for heads. Cover with newspaper strips, paper toweling and finally sheeting which may be brightly colored, dipped in laundry starch or white glue. (See Maps.) Faces can be left plain or have features added. If any Styrofoam is exposed, be sure that your paint will not melt it.

Pulp Method

Papier Mâché (cooked pulp method)

Modern newspapers do not break down into pulp easily, so we recommend that you always plan to use the cooked pulp recipe given here.

4 cups   torn newspaper (1 inch square or less)
¼ cup   dry wallpaper (wheat) paste
1 cup water

Tear newspaper into small pieces and place in a large container or bucket. Soak in water for a day and bring to a boil in a pan for one hour. Cool. Work the wet paper into a pulp by hand to squeeze out excess water and remove lumps. Place pulp in a large container. Make a creamy mixture of wallpaper paste and water, stirring out all the lumps. The paste should be of mayonnaise consistency. Mix pulp and paste together until the pulp has the consistency of cookie dough. All proportions can be increased for larger amounts.

Use the mixture immediately or keep it in a covered plastic container. One-half teaspoon of oil of wintergreen may be added to help keep the pulp sweet.

When molded, dry objects in an oven at 250° F. or in the sun. Set on a rack so that air can get to the base.

If the project involves only small amounts of papier mâché pulp—such as in adding hair, eyebrows and facial features to give depth to the strip method—you may want to use a small amount of the instant papier mâché.

Use pulp papier mâché as a modeling compound to cover surfaces, to mold shapes and to give textures. Allow sufficient drying time; then sand, if necessary. Finally, paint the object.

PHOTOGRAPHY (see Cameras)

pictures

WHAT THEY ARE—

We include here original art works, reproductions or art prints, photographs and completed drawings (for the process, see Drawing). We exclude all non-representational art works, such as abstract art, since children are less likely to use pictures that they cannot clearly relate to something they are studying.

WHEN AND WHERE TO USE THEM—

Children use pictures when they want to see something that someone else has created to represent a particular subject. In addition, children will use pictures when they simply want to enjoy their beauty.

Pictures can be used in any setting, indoors or outdoors, in which they can be viewed. They should be hung at the children's eye level if they are displayed on a wall. Sometimes they may be used and handled by the children, rather than displayed on a wall or bulletin board.

WHY CHILDREN USE THEM—

Pictures allow children to:
—enlarge their own personal experience by developing a mental picture of something they have not actually experienced
—find a way to represent an object, idea or event
—develop a story and share it through visuals
—relate ideas and feelings through visual representations
—Stimulate their own imagination and creativity.

WHAT CHILDREN NEED—

—carefully chosen art representations
—pictures that show life in other cultures
—pictures that provide background information

—pictures that are authentic to a period or situation or person

—opportunity to use pictures in a variety of ways in addition to viewing—as puzzles, topics for conversation, comparison, research, etc.

HOW TO USE THEM—

Teaching pictures and visuals of all types should be evaluated as to how well they help children learn. How do they involve the children? What do they add to their concept of the physical world? Evaluate each picture on the basis of the following kinds of questions:

1. *Purpose.* What is my purpose in using this picture with children—to stimulate emotion? To portray a time or event in the past? To give visual input to a verbal message? To provide items for comparison?

2. *Content.* Does the content of the picture relate directly to my purposes? Or is it not quite on target? Is the content true to our best understanding of what the time and place was actually like? Does this picture give any false information to children?

3. *Overall organization or composition.* Does the picture have a center of interest, with the remaining elements supporting the main thought or idea? Or is the total picture confusing and disorganized for children?

4. *Size.* Is the size of the picture right for the way I want to use it? For larger groups try to find larger pictures. If pictures are to be handled directly by children they can be smaller than if they are to be mounted on a wall for viewing.

5. *Color.* Does the color contribute to the main idea of the picture or does it detract from or confuse the message?

To help children really learn from pictures, it may be helpful to provide several interpretations of a scene or subject, if possible. To help girls and boys study a particular artist's work, you will need to provide more than one picture by that artist. Thus, a group or series of pictures will be most helpful in giving a whole view of a particular subject, of a certain artist, or of a certain style of art.

PICTURES

As children view pictures, some questions may be helpful:

What catches your eye first?
What is the main idea in the picture?
What feeling do you get from the picture?
When did the scene in this picture take place?
What might have happened just before this picture?
What might happen next?
What does the background tell you?
What do you think the artist is trying to tell us?
What does this picture tell us about the artist? about how he/she feels? about his/her faith? about how he/she looks at the world?

Using Pictures With Children

1. *Young Children.* Pictures used by younger children should not distort reality and should use a minimum of symbolism. The young child is working constantly at clarifying his or her understanding of the real world and his or her relationship to it. A picture should help in this process. Try to use pictures that represent something in the child's own experiences or where at least part of the picture will be familiar—pictures of families doing various things, of children with adults, scenes in the outdoors, animals and pictures of children doing things your children like to do.

Pictures will be most meaningful when children can do more than simply view them. Many teachers mount pictures on cardboard or colored construction paper and laminate the front with transparent self-stick plastic so that young children can carry them around without damaging them. Pictures can be mounted on cardboard cubes or boxes (using one picture on each side) in related sets, so that conversations can be stimulated as the cube is held, handled and carried around. Pictures can be made into jigsaw puzzles by mounting and laminating them and cutting them into puzzle pieces. Pictures can be used along with a story or a record or tape.

2. *Older Children.* When possible, display more than one picture on a subject and give the girls and boys opportunity to tell how they feel about the various pictures. Have them share which picture they think

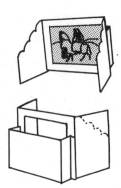

does the best job of telling a story, showing a setting or creating a feeling. Stress that we do not all have to like the same pictures, but that we should all have reasons why we do or do not like pictures. These reasons may not always be verbalized, but help children be aware of their existence. Children should also know that we do not have to like all of any particular picture. We may like parts of a number of pictures and not all of any of them.

When studying a picture showing a still scene, older children may pantomime the scene as they see it. This can be done simply, without costumes. Or costumes and minimum background settings could be added.

Another way of displaying pictures is to use the Japanese technique known as the Kamishibai theater. A series of pictures is displayed in a holder made so that one can be removed at a time in sequence. Make a frame out of heavy poster board or cardboard. Add a "pocket" at the back to hold the pictures and arrange a stand to keep the frame upright (see illustration). The pictures are placed in order in the frame, and as a story is told, the first one is removed to reveal the second picture. As the story progresses, all the pictures are displayed in order.

3. *An Art Display.* Help boys and girls collect many pictures of various episodes in the life of Jesus or some other subject. Try to include pictures by artists of many cultures. Display these and give the children an opportunity to react to them. They may want to choose their favorite ones.

4. *A Picture File.* Work out a system to store your pictures. It is as important to care properly for the pictures when they are not in use as it is to have them readily available when we need them. Choose a large sturdy box with cardboard dividers, or use a special picture filing cabinet. A list of suggested subject headings for such a file is available from Cokesbury Church Library Service.*

---

* "Learning Resource Filing System" (#426-E). Available from Cokesbury Church Library Service, 201 Eighth Avenue, South, Nashville, TN 37202.

5. *Display Pictures.* Use a wide variety of ways. Investigate the many things you can do with large pieces of cardboard (such as box lids). Make a triptych (a display area with three sections) if you have pictures that represent events happening in a certain order. For a larger grouping, tape together a number of cardboard pieces in an accordion arrangement. Pictures can then be mounted in proper sequence on all the pieces. If desired, you can mount pictures on both sides.

plaques

WHAT IT IS—

A plaque is a thin, flat plate or tablet of metal, porcelain, wood, cardboard, plaster, etc., intended to be hung as a wall decoration.

WHEN AND WHERE TO DO IT—

Children can make plaques any time they wish to create a decorative wall hanging, either as a gift or as a way of preserving some design or object(s).

Children may gather items to use in plaques in many places. Actual preparation needs to be done in a place where the background surface can be prepared (plaster poured and allowed to dry or wood cut and smoothed) and the design either drawn or mounted. The job should be done in a place where undisturbed drying time will be possible, if needed.

WHY CHILDREN DO IT—

Plaques allow children to—
—discover objects of beauty that are worth preserving
—prepare something of beauty to share with someone else
—make judgments about the design of something that is pleasing to them.

93

WHAT CHILDREN NEED—

—clay, dough or modeling mixture (for younger children); (see recipe for cooked play-dough in Clay Modeling, and for salt clay or Great Stuff in Beads)
—plaster of Paris mixture (see Carving for recipe) and old saucer
—pieces of plywood or weathered boards (sanded smooth around edges)
—pieces of cardboard or poster board
—nature objects: pebbles, leaves, nuts, seeds, pods, wheat, twigs, etc.
—old pictures, wrapping paper, greeting cards, etc.
—adhesive: white glue
—paints: poster or tempera, acrylics
—carbon paper
—stain: brown liquid shoe polish
—wood seal: paste wax, clear spray fixative (optional)
—hooks: hair pins, paper clips, picture-hanging rings or ribbon.

HOW TO DO IT—

Children can make many different kinds of plaques, depending on their interests, abilities and purposes. The following instructions will give you some ideas:

1. *Handprint Plaque.* This is a natural for very young children. Use earth clay, dough, or one of the other modeling mixtures. Start out with a piece of clay approximately ½ inch thick, and mark out a circle with a plate or saucer. Excess clay can be cut off with a dull knife or popsicle stick and the edge smoothed. The child then presses his or her hand down into the center of the clay. Be sure that all the fingers are pressed well down, since the tendency is to push hardest with the palm of the hand. After the handprint is made, insert a hook (hair pin or paper clip) while the clay is damp. Or make two small holes with a large nail for hanging with a ribbon. Painting is optional. The handprint alone can be painted, or the area around the print. With younger children it may be best to leave the plaque unpainted.

2. *Pasted Picture Plaque.* Another simple plaque for young children can be made with pictures cut from

story papers or student books, greeting cards, magazines. Cut out a piece of cardboard or poster board the same size and shape as the picture. Glue the picture down with white glue; when dry, a protective finish can be added by painting a light coat of diluted glue over the picture. Glue gold cord or gift tie around the edges of the cardboard, first making a loop for hanging by tying a knot. Place this loop at the center top and glue cord around both sides of the plaque.

Older children may wish to try this method on wood. Cut a piece of plywood or ½-inch-thick wood large enough so that there will be a wood frame showing all around the picture. The wood should be sanded so that all corners and edges are smooth, and may or may not be covered with a light wash of diluted tempera paint. Glue the picture in place and add a hanging, either the screw-type brass ring or the ribbon tied through two drilled holes.

3. *Wood Pretties.* Many children who like to glue things will enjoy making these plaques, which originated among descendants of the English, Scotch, Irish, and Pennsylvania German settlers in Tennessee, Kentucky, Georgia, Alabama and the Carolinas. Called "Wood Pretties," these are made by arranging on a piece of wood dried seeds, grasses, burrs, pods, acorns, leaves, berries, etc. Either sanded plywood or clean weathered boards can be used. Staining can be done with a light wash of watered tempera or with liquid brown shoe polish, or the wood may be used in its natural color. Some people also like to apply paste wax to the surface of the wood to seal it; two coats, allowed to dry and then polished, are usually enough. Children can arrange and rearrange the dried nature objects as they wish—let them make the design! Once the design is completed, each piece is glued onto the plaque. Attach a hanging ring or ribbon.

4. *Nature Plaque.* Make a plaque out of plaster of Paris and place the seeds, pods, leaves, twigs, etc. in the plaster. Pour plaster into a mold you have lined with waxed paper, so that the plaster can be removed when dry. Or pour the plaster directly onto a piece of plywood or cardboard, so that when dry it will stick to the wood or cardboard, which provides a

"frame." Children arrange their nature items in the wet plaster and add a hanging loop (hair pin or paper clip) at the same time.

5. *Japanese Porcelain Plaque.* The Japanese make lovely porcelain plaques as decorations. Children can reproduce the Japanese "lotus blossom" design shown here or make their own design. Pour plaster of Paris mixture into an old saucer that has been wet with water to keep the plaster from sticking. Fill the saucer and let it dry for about 45 minutes. While the plaster is setting, children can prepare their designs on paper. Help them keep their designs simple. Remind them that the final design can be in more than one color. When the plaster is hard, children can place a hand (palm down) on the plaque and twist gently to loosen it from the saucer in one piece. Any edges that crumble can be smoothed with a knife or nail file. Now have the children transfer their designs from paper to plaster with carbon paper and ball point pen.

Painting comes next, and you may want to suggest that the children experiment first, either on the back of the plaques or on some other pieces of dried plaster. With poster or tempera paint, the less water in the paint, the more "build-up" children can achieve and the less water there will be to soak into the plaster. With acrylic paint there should be little soaking in, and the paint should dry quickly. If the children have decided to use more than one color, caution them about applying two wet colors adjacent to each other. Wet paints will run.

plastics

WHAT THEY ARE—

Plastics are manufactured materials that come in almost any form, color, and in almost any texture or hardness, varying from a hardness like steel to the softness of silk. The word *plastics* comes from the Greek word *plastikos,* meaning "able to be molded."

Children will probably most use plastics recycled from some other source. This includes packaging materials and pieces of Styrofoam from cartons and boxes.

WHEN AND WHERE TO USE THEM—

Children can use plastics for construction, collage, recycling, as well as for bases for wire sculptures or stabiles. These plastic materials can be used anywhere.

WHY CHILDREN USE THEM—

Plastics allow children to:
—increase their appreciation of, and find new uses for, everyday materials
—find ways to recycle household items
—create new things with liquid plastics that harden.

WHAT CHILDREN NEED—

—previously used plastics:
  —old plastic toys
  —containers of all kinds (bottles, jugs, bowls, cups, glasses, etc.)
  —packaging materials (trays from meats, dividers, egg cartons, small pieces shaped like peanuts and/ or thick spaghetti, etc.)
—tools for cutting plastics:
  —scissors, serrated kitchen knife, coping saw
  —a heated wire cutter for large Styrofoam pieces
—colored plastic toothpicks
—paper punch
—white glue (lightly sand the area to be glued to help the two surfaces to adhere)
—liquid resin plastic and its hardening solution
—coloring compound (one brand is trademarked "Boss Gloss")

HOW TO USE THEM—

Children can do many projects using plastics, including collage and construction. The following are examples.

97

1. *Fun Dings*. Save all kinds of Styrofoam packing pieces and ask at the china and dishware department in local stores to see if they receive their merchandise packed in the little Styrofoam pieces that look like peanuts or thick spaghetti.

Young children can make constructions with colored plastic toothpicks and Styrofoam pieces. Encourage children to create their own designs. For added color they can attach small shapes of construction paper with the toothpicks.

2. *Three-D Plastic Collage*. Use a heavy cardboard as the base for a collage containing bits and pieces of plastic of all colors, sizes and shapes. Old toys can be taken apart and the pieces used separately. To attach large pieces, push two holes through the cardboard and loop a pipe cleaner around the object and through to the back. Children can also use white glue to keep items in place. Encourage experimentation with size, color, shape and texture.

3. *Recycle Those Containers*. Many plastic bottles, jugs, etc. can be made into useful items. To cut the container, fill it with hot water and let stand about ten minutes. Empty and cut while the plastic is softened. Use a sharp utility knife to make a slit and then large scissors. An awl or nail will make holes. Decorate with adhesive-backed vinyl, colored vinyl tapes or permanent felt markers.

One simple project for children is an Indian belt. The medallions are cut from detergent bottles and the designs are made with permanent felt markers. Use medium weight white cord.

Plastic from containers can also be used for name tags, pieces for mobiles, for small signs and for small information cards. Also, children can use detergent bottles to make small easels on which to stand their favorite pictures.

4. *Styrofoam*. When using large pieces of molded foam and the Styrofoam sheets you will sometimes want to add color. Most spray paints contain a chemical that causes the foam to "melt." One product that will not do this is known as "Boss Gloss" and is produced by the California Titan Products, Inc., Santa Ana, California. This product can also be used on

easel

unbaked clay, plaster of Paris and ceramic tile. *CAUTION:* Never burn Styrofoam—it gives off a harmful gas when burned.

5. *Liquid Plastic.* Liquid resin, sold under a number of different trade names, requires addition of both a coloring and a hardener. Always follow directions carefully. Molds can be purchased in different sizes and shapes, but it is also fun to find your own.

Older elementary children enjoy making plastic medallions. Plastic coffee can lids or those used to seal smaller cans will make good molds. The symbol can be arranged in the lid, using pieces of colored glass, stones or small pieces of wood. Glue in place on the plastic lid. When the glue is dry, mix up the liquid resin, including the hardener, and pour it into the lid around the symbol. When dry, push the medallion out from the plastic lid. Other small nature items can be imbedded in plastic in the same way. If the medallion is to hang on a string or chain, be sure you glue in place a piece of toothpick or drinking straw to provide the hole after the resin has dried.

Another project is the creation of small vases or paperweights, using heavy duty aluminum foil as the mold. Crumple the foil lightly to make it into the shape you want. For a bud vase, shape foil around a small glass jar (such as medicine or vitamins come in). For a paperweight, let the foil create its own shape. Pour the liquid resin into the foil and let it harden. Remove the foil before the resin gets completely cold and hard. *Note:* Do not crinkle the foil too much or it will be difficult to pull away from the hardened plastic.

playwriting

WHAT IT IS—

Playwriting is the process of writing a story in dialogue form that can be acted and/or read aloud.

99

Playwriting is for older children. All children, especially young children, should have many opportunities for informal creative dramatics (see Acting Out/Drama) before attempting written dialogue.

WHEN AND WHERE TO DO IT—

Children enjoy taking the parts of other persons or animals in a drama and usually enjoy telling a story in dramatic form. When they want to write down their dialogue, they will use the playwriting process. Playwriting can be fun in any setting. Children need a place to write, and sometimes they will want to try acting out their ideas as they write them down.

WHY CHILDREN DO IT—

Playwriting allows children to:
—share with others how characters react in certain situations
—portray in dramatic form a story they have enjoyed
—express in dialogue format the feelings of others
—create a lifelike situation in story form.

WHAT CHILDREN NEED—

—lined paper and pencils
—time to think out the actions and words in a story
—stories to put in dramatic form (these may be stories they have had read to them or enjoyed reading themselves)
—adult leaders who:
   will help them work out the dialogue and actions in their stories
   will respect their ideas as important
   have a sense of the dramatic themselves.

HOW TO DO IT—

Children with limited experiences in playwriting should work on very simple, and fairly brief, stories or incidents. Help them succeed with a simple story, rather than get bogged down in a more difficult one.

Certain elements are necessary in developing a play:
Title
Time (When? What year? What season of year? Day or night?)

Setting (Where does it take place? What does it look like?)

Props (What is essential in clothing, scenery, etc.?)

Synopsis (Outline action from beginning to end.)

Characters (List and describe each.)

Work these matters out carefully before deciding on actual dialogue and action.

If the play is to be done informally, the characters can take the synopsis and make up the play as they go. But if the play is to have written dialogue, this is the next step in the process.

One method that may help is to have children talk the dialogue out first on the tape recorder. This way they can keep the action clearer in their minds and get the various speeches responding to one another in such a way as to keep the story moving. They will need help later in transcribing dialogue from the tape so that it can be refined and improved.

As children write down the speeches, explain why they should begin each speech on a separate line with the character's name to the left of the speech.

When the entire play has been written down, the children may want to arrange for a once-through oral reading, to check for sequence and flow of action and ideas, as well as speech.

Note: Once again, remember to keep such plays brief, so that children don't get bogged down in the mechanics of getting a long play down on paper.

poetry

WHAT IT IS—

Poetry involves words arranged in lines, usually with a regularly repeated rhythm or accent and sometimes with rhyme. Not all styles of poetry are enjoyed by children. Suggestions are given here for free verse, cinquain, haiku and limerick.

WHEN TO DO IT—

Children use poetry to express ideas that might never be expressed in conversation. Often poetry is created when children are having fun with words— seeing how many words they can think of that end with a certain sound or how many words describe an object, a feeling, or an event. Such experimenting, begun as a game, gives the children confidence that they can create with words. In this way poetry can begin as a group activity and later become an individual project.

WHERE TO DO IT—

Children can create poetry informally in any place where they are letting words suggest new words. They do this in their own conversations while singing, chattering, swinging, or while playing group games. The more formal writing of poetry should be done where paper and pencil can be used.

WHY CHILDREN DO IT—

Poetry allows children to:
—express their ideas
—use words in fun, especially in rhymes and limericks
—communicate a feeling, wondering, thought, or worry
—experience the wonders of language
—develop respect for the written word
—develop ability to use verbal skills
—choose words carefully to express meaning
—experience the satisfaction of seeing their words in written form and of hearing their words being read.

WHAT CHILDREN NEED—

—lined paper and pencils
—larger paper (for those who may want to display a poem)
—adult leaders who:
    provide an accepting atmosphere
    respect the written word
    will give reassurance that children's ideas are worthy of sharing

will provide the opportunity for children to experiment with words.

HOW TO DO IT—

Many teachers of young children keep a tablet and pencil within easy reach so that they can "capture" the spontaneously poetic words of their children.

Children naturally emphasize repetition. One way they can do this is to create 5 or 10 lines of poetry, each beginning with the same first words: I wish . . . ; Christmas is . . . ; The church is . . . ; Indians . . . .

Other simple poems by young children may be two lines in length and may be about something that is important to them, like: my kitten, home, my family, I have a tricycle, etc.

Older children have some beginning writing skills. As they begin thinking through some of their ideas, they may want to test them out with someone else. Help older children use the skills they have already learned—using the dictionary, recalling their previous experiences with poetry and word games.

1. *Free Verse.* Free verse can be written down in a variety of forms. The lines can be as short as one word, or of any length. The words may be written on a page in such a way that they themselves create a shape, like an egg, a Christmas tree, a leaf, a footprint, or almost any shape. Here the visual arrangement helps to carry the message of the poem.

2. *Cinquain (sin CANE).* From France comes a poetic form that has five lines. Beginning with one word, the first four lines increase from one to four words; then the last line repeats the one-word form. The words must fit certain other requirements, as follows:

Line 1	Title (a noun; one word)	<u>God</u>
Line 2	Describes the title (two words)	<u>great</u> <u>creator</u>
Line 3	Action words (verbs) or a phrase about the title; (three words)	<u>acting</u> <u>for</u> <u>persons</u>

Line 4 Describes a feeling <u>always</u> <u>willing</u> <u>to</u> <u>forgive</u>
about the title
(four words)

Line 5 A word that means   <u>Love</u>
the same as the
title (one word)

This form can also be adapted so that the lines are formed with two words, four words, six words, eight words, and two words.

3. *Haiku*. This Japanese poetic form captures a single moment of awareness or a single impression. There are three elements in haiku—time, place and object. Children will be able to grow in their ability to select words skillfully to give meaning to each of these elements. Often the poem is an expression of nature or the seasons, and the reader is expected to bring feelings and understandings to add to the words that are written.

A haiku poem has seventeen syllables in three lines. The first line has five syllables, the second has seven and the last has five. Try writing one that expresses your feeling about winter sky, blossoms, a bird in flight.

This haiku poem was written by a third grade boy:

>   The witches scare on
>   Hallowe'en night, black cats prowl,
>   . ghosts haunt everywhere.

4. *Limerick*. This five-line story ends with a surprise. The lines follow a certain pattern of syllables and rhyme that give the poem movement when it is read. These lines also advance the story in a patterned way:

Line 1 — — — — — — — — (8 syllables) (Rhyme A)   Introduces the character of the story.

Line 2 — — — — — — — — (8 syllables) (Rhyme A) ⎫
Give the character something to do.
Line 3 — — — — — (5 syllables) (Rhyme B) ⎬
Line 4 — — — — — (5 syllables) (Rhyme B) ⎭

Line 5 — — — — — — — — (8 syllables) (Rhyme A) End with the surprise.

Make a list of words that rhyme. This provides some variety as the boys and girls then try to form the lines,

using some of those words. This will be especially helpful in coming up with the last line, which has the surprise ending.

As an example, see what a fifth grader did:

There was a young astronaut who
Went rocketing into the blue.
But as he shot off
He started to cough
And caught a bad case of the flu.

posters

WHAT THEY ARE—

A poster is a communication tool with a single message, usually placed on paper, using words alone or words and pictures.

WHEN AND WHERE TO USE THEM—

Children can use posters to announce an event or convey an idea—when they want to give out information and ask persons to respond. For example:
—for a clothing drive, use clothing shapes cut from cloth
—for a Mexican fiesta, use the bright warm colors of that culture
—for a Bible quote (or other writing), use a border design or a shape of a scroll.
Posters are often placed on bulletin boards, walls, telephone poles, in hallways and in store windows.

WHY CHILDREN USE THEM—

Posters allow children to:
—communicate one idea in simple form
—let others know about something important
—develop their skills in designing, drawing, lettering
—work together to decide how best to convey an idea.

WHAT CHILDREN NEED—

—heavy construction paper or poster board (15" x 20" or 20" x 30")
—construction paper in many colors
—felt markers, crayons, poster paints, brushes
—rulers, pencils, scissors, white glue
—pictures (if these are part of the design)
—three-dimensional materials (folded paper, plastic flowers, pipe cleaner figures, etc.)

HOW TO MAKE THEM—

Children need to keep these things in mind:
—everything in a poster should help it communicate
—a poster should have one or two central figures or objects; all other elements must be keyed to these central figures in size, shape, color and design
—choose colors that help communicate the one idea.

Help children write down their message. Then help them choose the main ideas—what do you want to emphasize? Decide who the message is beamed to—children? youth? all ages? Next, decide what colors will help attract attention. Then decide where the poster will be placed. Will it be on a stand? Hung? Mounted? Indoors or outdoors (outdoors takes weather-proof paints)? Will it be well lighted (poor lighting requires brighter colors)? What type of letters will best carry the message?

Have the children make several rough drawings and decide on the one that best tells their message. Then they can sketch lightly on the poster paper to show where letters and shapes will be. When they feel comfortable with the spacing, they can begin to color in the areas. Suggest that they check again at this point. Does the poster speak its message? Have the children complete the posters and erase the light pencil lines if they show. Of course, if other elements, like three-dimensional objects, are a part of the design, these should be added in their proper places. Finally, the children can hang posters at the proper eye level.

Note: Magazines and advertisements will be a constant source of ideas and designs. Collect pictures and layouts you especially like and begin an idea file.

Basic principles of good posters include: simplicity, appropriateness, attractiveness, design and color, contrast, center of interest, originality, proper size, and good use of color.

Some other variations: posters can be used on church bulletin boards, spatter painting can be done around lettering, silk screening process can be used for a large number of identical posters, mimeographed handouts can be used for a quick announcement.

See also Banners and Exhibit.

WHERE TO GET MORE HELP—

Wright, Leo, *Postercraft*. New York: Sterling Publishing Company, 1971. 64 pp.

pottery

WHAT IT IS—

Pottery refers to objects formed out of earth clay.

WHEN TO DO IT—

Making pottery will be especially useful when children are studying how persons of other times and other cultures have used this ancient skill. Having learned some simple skills themselves, children can try their hand at making pottery objects of their own.

WHERE TO DO IT—

Children need a flat, level surface on which to work, in a place that can easily be cleaned up after the work is done or between work sessions. Water should be available, both for moistening the clay and for handwashing.

Note: Most potters suggest washing hands in a bucket of water for at least two reasons: excess clay can be saved and re-used when it has settled in the bottom of the bucket, and washing clay into the drains of sinks can eventually cause plumbing problems!

WHY CHILDREN DO IT—

Pottery allows children to:
—begin to experience the "feel" of a medium that responds to the user's fingers
—experiment with a medium that is flexible and that can be re-used.
—create a new and original object of their own design
—reproduce their own version of items created by persons whom they have been studying.

WHAT CHILDREN NEED—

—a pliable clay material to work with; most preferable is a good earth clay. This can be a self-hardening type. You will need to search your area for the best outlets.
—a flat, level working surface
—some simple tools: table knife for smoothing or trimming, table fork or popsicle sticks for making designs, buckets and water for moistening clay and cleaning up, dampened rags or pieces of plastic for keeping clay moist
—paints and brushes to use for decorations

SOME HINTS ABOUT EARTH CLAY—

1. Earth clay has at least two variations: (1) the moist clay, which must be kept moist in airtight containers when not in use, and damp and moist when being worked, and (2) the self-hardening clay, which has a special drier added. This clay dries very hard and does not need to be baked.

2. Wedging should be done each time the clay is used to remove air bubbles and assure an even consistency. Follow these steps to "wedge" the clay:
—Make a rectangular shape of clay in your hands and throw it down hard on a board or table.
—Cut the clay in half with a piece of piano wire or fishing line. Each time you cut the clay, check the inside part to see that it has no air bubbles and that the inside of the clay has a smooth consistency throughout.
—Slam the two pieces of clay together with the cut sides out. Then push the two pieces together.

—Do this again and again. Throw it down hard; cut it in half; slam it together. Keep doing this until the clay is just right for working.

3. The clay must be at the right degree of moisture for working. If it is too wet and sticky, put it on a *dry* board and roll, twist and press until it is just right. If too dry, punch holes in it and squirt water into the holes. Then put the clay on a damp board and roll and knead until soft. For just a little softening, sprinkle water on the clay and work it in. If the clay is completely dry, mash with a rolling pin into powder and mix with water until it is like pancake batter. Be sure to stir it until you get out all the lumps, but stir slowly so you do not work a lot of air bubbles into the mixture. Then wait until the water evaporates; during this time keep turning and pressing the clay so a crust does not form on it. When it is soft and pliable, store in a covered container. Between work sessions keep the clay in an airtight container or plastic bag; be sure to cover any unfinished projects with a damp cloth or plastic.

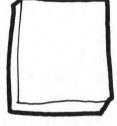

4. To add new pieces of soft clay (for ears, noses, buttons, etc.) to clay that is already hard, follow these steps:

—*Slowly* sponge the hard clay with your damp cloth or sponge until it feels soft again.

—With your fingernail or a stick, scratch ("score") the surfaces where the clay is to be joined, making them rough.

—Make a creamy mixture of clay and water; this is called "slip." Spread a layer of slip over both surfaces.

—Press the two pieces together firmly but gently and hold for a minute until you are sure they will stick.

5. Dry the object in the air at room temperature. Place on a rack so air can get to the under side of large pieces. This is the end of the process with self-hardening clay. With regular earth clay, the dry object can then be fired in a kiln.

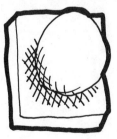

HOW TO DO IT—

Here are some simple suggestions for ways children can use earth clay to make figures, dishes, vases, etc.

1. Children can use four simple beginning shapes: brick, ball, link and slab.

a. *Brick.* Use a rectangular clay shape and draw an outline (on one side) of whatever you wish to make. Cut away the extra clay along that line, so that the form begins to take shape but is still squarish. Now, pressing gently and firmly, begin to model the square form to make it round. Gradually it will take the desired form.

b. *Ball.* Start with a lump of clay. By twisting, squeezing and shaping, the form begins to take shape.

c. *Links.* Begin with long fat rolls of clay. These can either be cut in half lengthwise and rolled again, or the fat rolls can be rolled some more until smaller. Forms are made by cutting the rolls into various sizes, like sausage links, and attaching them to one another by means of the scoring and slipping process. The final figure or form can then be shaped and molded.

d. *Slab.* Roll out a lump of clay with a rolling pin or bottle as you would pie crust. Draw and cut out the figure you want. You can bend and shape the figure, make it stand, sit or run.

2. These basic forms can be used to make more complicated creations, like figures, dishes, vases and pots.

a. *Making People with the Ball and Link Method.* Roll the clay into a coil about as thick as a broom handle. Cut a piece long enough to make the legs of your figure and bend into a horseshoe shape. Cut a shorter piece to form the trunk of the body and join it to the legs. Make the head out of a ball of clay and attach. Then attach another link for the arms by adding it to the chest and by pushing firmly into the body. Be sure to score each surface and use the creamy paste clay (slip) to attach the pieces.

b. *Making People with the Pinch and Pull Method.* Make a ball of clay. Squeeze one end until you have made an egg-shaped piece for the head. Punch and pull out two more for the arms and then two more for the legs. Use fingers and both hands to press and pull the clay until it is solid and you have the shape you want. Children can press and pull all kinds of figures —animals, birds, etc.—in the same way.

c. Using the Pinch Method to Make a Vase, Dish or Pot. Use a ball of fine-grained and very pliable clay. Support the ball on the palm of one hand and press downward on the exact top and center of the ball with the thumb of your other hand. As your thumb goes into the center of the ball, bring your fingers down against the outside surface in a pinching motion. Keep turning the ball with the supporting hand and pinching with the other hand. As you turn the clay, keep pinching and shaping the sides until they are the desired thickness and proper shape. For larger dishes and bowls, you will need to use thumbs and fingers of both hands for the pinching and shaping process; placing the clay on a piece of paper allows it to turn freely on a flat surface during the shaping.

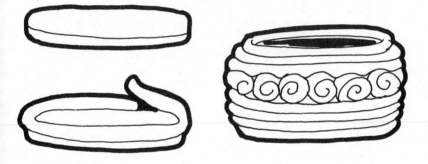

d. Using the Coil Method to Make a Vase, Dish or Pot. Make a base by rolling out a piece of clay at least ¼ inch thick. Cut it to the shape you want with a dull knife. Make coils by rolling clay on a damp surface under the fingers of both hands. Cut and place the first one so that it fits around the edge of the base. After scoring and slipping, lay the first coil of clay around the edge of the base. As you continue, you can determine the shape of the bowl or pot by the position of each new coil. To make the walls go out, lay each row on the outer edge of the previous row; to go in, use the inner edge. Smooth each coil of clay on the inside. The outside can be either smooth or retain the design of the coils themselves.

111

This process is used in reproducing various types of Indian pottery. This bowl, for example, shows the shape and decorative design made by the Zuni Indians. Many of the early cliff dwellers made designs almost completely in black and white, but later the Zunis and other tribes of the southwest added colors made from different clays and soils. The Indians used leaves from the yucca plant to make their paint brushes. Some of the best Indian pottery was made in the southwestern part of the United States.

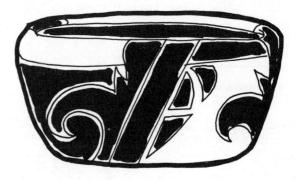

Oriental Decoration for Pottery. Since it is believed that pottery originated in China as early as 3000 B.C., you and your children may be interested in using some Oriental decorations. For instance, your children may want to use the four flowers that symbolize the four seasons of the year:

spring	peony
summer	lotus
autumn	chrysanthemum
winter	flowering plum

The lotus is also the sacred flower of Buddha.

The iris is often used in Asian pottery because it stands for the sword, or strength. The dragon stands for supernatural power and is also the personal symbol of the Emperor.

You and your children may want to do some special study into the various designs that have been used on pottery by many of the peoples of the world.

See also Clay Modeling.

prints & printing

WHAT IT IS—

Printing is the process of using inked shapes to put designs, patterns, letters or words on another surface. Even young children can enjoy printing with shapes cut from vegetables. Older children can design intricate patterns for producing items like stationery, cards, books and decorated cloth.

WHEN AND WHERE TO DO IT—

Children can use printing to create interesting new patterns and designs on cloth or paper even before cutting skills are acquired. They can do printing wherever there is a flat work surface, either indoors or out.

WHY CHILDREN DO IT—

Printing—or the making of prints—allows children to:
—reproduce shapes, designs and textures they have created themselves
—develop an understanding of the concept of positive-negative, i.e. the printed design is the opposite of the object created to make the design
—produce simple designs before they are able to cut out complicated patterns.

WHAT CHILDREN NEED—

This is a general listing. More specific items are given with each detailed procedure below.
—tempera paint
—tubes of water color ink (oil does not wash up with water and takes longer to dry)
—textile paint for block printing on fabric
—typing paper or other lightweight paper
—newspaper (for padding)

—cardboard
—knife (to cut potatoes, art gum erasers, etc.)
—line printing roller or brayer (one for each child)
—smooth flat surface (piece of glass, pieces of Masonite, flat plastic dinner plate)
—a drying line with clip-type clothes pins (for drying prints)
—materials for making designs (cork; foam plastic; feathers; bottle caps; cans; jar bottoms and tops; corrugated cardboard; wood; flat plaster plaques; keys; combs; strings; cords; vegetables such as potatoes, carrots, turnips, lettuce, cabbage; fabrics with heavy texture such as burlap, coarse linen, lace; nature items such as leaves, grasses with a wide variety of sizes and shapes; children's wooden alphabet blocks—with the exception of B, F, G, J, K, L, P, Q, and R, which would print backwards; commercially available printing sets).

HOW TO DO IT—

Printing With Young Children. With simple printing, children can create lovely wrapping paper. They may use metal cookie cutters dipped in tempera paint and placed on shelf paper in a random design. Varying the color of the tempera paint also provides some choices as children finish one piece of paper and start another.

Or use fruits and vegetables sliced through the middle so that the entire flat surface is put in the paint and then printed on the paper. Children might try carrots, potatoes, turnips, radishes, bell peppers, beets, cabbage, oranges, apples and grapes.

Another approach for young children involves rolling paint on an object to make a print. Collect flat nature items, such as leaves and grasses. While they are still pliable, coat one side with paint, using a roller or brayer. Then place a piece of paper over the object and press with your hand or a clean roller. This will create a print on the paper.

Cutting Certain Shapes. Vegetable printing can be adapted so that only certain shapes are printed. The design should be simple (circles, diamonds, triangles, straight lines either parallel or as rays from the sun,

114

etc.) so that the portion of vegetable that prints is substantial. After slicing the vegetable in two, use a sharp pencil to draw the design on one piece. Then use a paring knife to cut around the outline of the design and to cut away (about ¼ inches deep) all but the design itself. Place a small amount of tempera paint or water color printing ink in a flat dish. To print, the child inks the raised portion and then presses it onto the paper.

Finger Painting Print. After a child has made a finger painting (see Painting), pull a print off that design by lightly placing another piece of paper over it and peeling it off immediately.

Fingerprint Art. Put some colored tempera on a small sponge or a pad of dampened paper towel. Now ink the fingertips and press them onto paper. Help the children discover how they can make bunches of grapes by placing a number of fingerprints close together. Other designs include flowers, owls, chickens and other animals. Use a felt marker to outline the animal or design.

Scratched Designs. Put some paint (or printing ink) on a piece of glass about 10 inches square. Use a roller or brayer to spread the ink evenly. Then use the eraser end of a pencil or other dull object to draw a design or picture on the inked surface. Lay a piece of paper across the glass, press lightly and peel off.

Exploring Textures and Surfaces. Spread ink on such items as textured cloth, wire screen, lace, corrugated cardboard, dried glue designs. Press down a piece of paper and then lift it off.

Flat Designs. Children can make surfaces that can be printed many times. One method involves making a design by gluing smaller pieces of cardboard onto a large piece of heavy cardboard. Remember that the design must be arranged so that it is backward from the printing desired. Ink only the raised surfaces, using a roller or brayer, and don't use too much ink. Lay down paper, press and lift. Ink again between each printing. Or make a design by gluing pieces of twine, cord or string onto a large piece of cardboard. Older children can create more intricate designs by planning more than one surface to be inked. Then they can use

a different colored ink with each one. This means that each print is done first with one color, allowed to dry, and then done with a second color.

Printing Sets. Inexpensive commercial printing sets for children allow them to make words and shapes for simple announcements and handbills.

Block Printing. By far the most intricate kind of printing activity mentioned here is block printing. Purchase linoleum blocks, usually about 6 x 8 inches, from hobby stores or school suppliers. You will need a set of linoleum block tools or wood carving tools, block printing ink, a brayer the width of the block.

Make a simple design and draw it on the block. Keep lines and sections thick and wide. If you are using words or a design that has a right or left side, remember that the design needs to be drawn on the block backwards. For example, the letter "B" should be drawn 𝐁 on the block, and "boy" would be drawn 𝐁𝐨𝐲 .

Use the cutting tools to remove the background of the design (unless you have created a design where the background prints and the design does not, as in a silhouette). Ink the design with the brayer, press down paper over the block and peel off. This type of block can make many copies.

This method is especially good for making notepaper, stationery, Christmas cards, booklet covers.

WHERE TO GET MORE HELP—

Cross, Jeanne, *Simple Printing Methods.* New York: S. G. Phillips, Inc., 1972. 47 pp.

puppets

WHAT THEY ARE—

Puppets are small figures that represent characters or persons and that can be manipulated dramatically.

The emphasis with children will usually be on *use* rather than *making* of the puppets. That is, the puppets will most often be used as a means of accomplishing certain learning goals.

WHEN TO USE THEM—

Puppets may be used when a dramatic approach to the study of a particular subject is appropriate, or when children simply want to enjoy drama through puppets. Since making puppets can take considerable time, depending on the type being made, leaders should plan their time schedule carefully. The types of puppets suggested here can be made fairly simply and quickly, and the children can spend their time enjoying and using them.

WHERE TO USE THEM—

Elaborate stage settings are unnecessary for many puppet activities, and often simple portable stages can be used in almost any situation. Puppets can be used both indoors and outdoors. In fact, the natural out-door setting would be desirable for certain stories.

To make puppets, certain materials and a good working space will be necessary. Table tops or large floor spaces will be helpful if many children are involved.

WHY CHILDREN USE THEM—

Puppets allow children to:
—act out in a new way a story, Scripture account, or play they are already familiar with
—engage in impromptu dialogue on various subjects
—forget their personal shyness and do their talking through a puppet
—think and act in the style of another person or an animal
—express at a deeper level than the verbal those ideas they are trying to understand
—think through the feelings and emotions of a character and decide how this is shown in body movement (in the puppet), approach to other characters, ways of talking, etc.
—entertain others by sharing plays and stories.

117

WHAT CHILDREN NEED—

—paper plates (do not use the plastic-coated kind)
—crayons, felt markers
—yarn, felt scraps, sewing trims
—fabric (large pieces in skin colors for bodies; large pieces for making clothing)
—unbleached muslin, white sheeting, or cotton fabric
—needles and thread
—construction paper
—pictures of persons from teaching pictures, catalogs or magazines
—sticks (rulers, unsharpened pencils, dowel rods)

HOW TO MAKE AND USE THEM—

We intentionally deal here with simple puppets that children can make easily and quickly so they can get on with using the puppets in plays and stories. For more information, use the book suggested at the end of this section.

A good rule for puppets, as for dolls, is the smaller the child, the larger and simpler the puppet. Most of your time should be spent in developing the story line and enjoying the adventures of the puppet figures.

Puppet Stages

The quickest puppet stage is a banquet table turned on its side with the legs opened up. The puppeteers sit on the floor behind the table and manipulate their puppets along its top edge.

Another quick stage can be made in an open doorway by taping or tacking up a large cloth sheet or piece of mural paper. For the stage opening, cut up the two sides and across the top to create a flap that will fold down. Before the performance, tape the flap up.

A more permanent wooden puppet stage can be built with three pieces of plywood or Masonite. The pieces are hinged together so that they stand up, and the stage hole is cut in the center piece. This stage will be most permanent and durable if each piece of wood is attached to a wooden frame, built around its edge and attached at the back. A curtain can be placed on a rod over the stage opening if desired. One or two children should then be able to sit on small chairs behind this stage as they operate the puppets.

Choosing and Preparing Stories

Many Bible stories, especially the Gospel stories, lend themselves to retelling by children in puppet plays. Children often find meaning for their own lives from the dialogue they create for their puppets. Stories from children's literature are often well suited to puppet plays. In addition, you can make up your own stories. Remember that puppets require lots of action.

When preparing a story for use with puppets, be familiar with the story. Make a brief outline of the action in the story; list the characters needed for each scene. Make the necessary puppets, and practice the story, using the puppets. Then share the puppet story with others.

How to Make Different Kinds of Puppets

1. *Paper Plate Puppets.* Fold a paper plate in half, and you immediately have a head with a huge mouth. Hold the puppet head at the fold to control the opening and closing of the mouth. Design ears, teeth, tongue, eyes and add them to the puppet head. Use scissors to cut a long beak or snout for certain animals or birds, or glue a beak or snout onto the paper plate. (See illustrations.)

Plates that have not been treated with plastic will best absorb tempera paints or colored felt markers. Exotic animals can be made by coloring the outside of the mouth one way and the inside another way. Or you can decorate the outside with spots, feathers, etc. Some puppeteers also sew up a fabric sleeve to cover their arm that matches the rest of the puppet.

Encourage the children to see how many different ways they can make their puppets talk and act.

2. *Stuffed Paper Bag Puppets.* Use grocery bags in sizes 4 to 6. Place your hand in the bag, hold it up and look at it. What can be done to make this into a puppet face? How can you make a neck? Hair? Facial features? Let the children decide on their own answers and then proceed to make their bags into quick puppets. Some children will want to make facial features with crayon or felt markers, hair with markers or by gluing on some yarn. The head begins to take shape when some rolled up newspaper is stuffed in and it is tied at the neck. (See illustration.) Allow room for the middle finger to extend up into the head and the little finger and thumb to come out through holes in the sides of the bag, thus providing arms for the puppet figure. The neck can be tied with a tie or a bow, and additional clothing can easily be sewed up and placed around the bag and arm below the neck. Be sure to cut armholes for finger and thumb. Or if arms and hands are included with the clothing, they should be stuffed with a light roll of newspaper to make them stiff.

3. *A Stick Puppet.* The paper bag puppet can be made into a large stick puppet by stuffing a large dowel rod up into the head and taping or tying it securely at the neck.

4. *A Bag Doll.* Another variation of the paper bag puppet, ideal for very young children, is a large paper bag doll that can be moved around and that can stand alone. Make the puppet head as explained above, using a size 4 bag. Then fill a number 6 bag one quarter full of sand, dirt or gravel to provide some weight. Seal shut with tape and place in the bottom of another number 6 bag. Use balls of newspaper (or shredded newspaper) to fill up the rest of the body bag to within about three inches of the top. Place the puppet head into the top of the body and tie it at the neck with a piece of string. Then wrap masking tape around the neck for a smooth surface. Dress this puppet-doll as desired. These will stand alone, and the younger children can move them around as they dramatize a story.

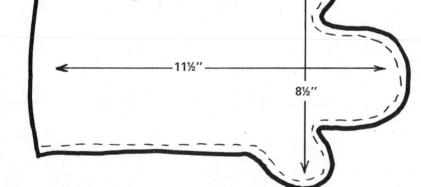

5. *A Quick Fabric Puppet.* Use the pattern above and cut out two shapes for each puppet, using unbleached muslin, sheeting or cotton fabric. Place the two pieces together, right side in, and machine sew around the edges. Leave the bottom open for the hand. Do this much before the class session, turning the puppets inside out so that the sewing seam will be on the inside.

Children can use crayons to draw facial features and hair (be sure they know they can decorate both front and back). They can also draw clothing—lines for a shirt, robe, fancy dress, or whatever is called for in the character. Children can make as many puppets as they need, plus a few extras. (*Note:* These also make excellent gifts for sick children or for friends.)

6. *Stick Puppet.* This type of puppet is easily made from figures the children draw themselves. Have them use pieces of paper 3 x 8½ inches. If they fill the paper with their figures, the puppets will all be about the same size. Cut out the figures and tape to a stick (dowel rod, ruler, pencil, etc.). Figures in teaching pictures and pictures in catalogs and magazines can also be used. This type of puppet can be moved easily, freeing the child to concentrate on the story line.

7. *Finger Puppet.* Finger puppets can be made of paper (as illustrated) or of felt. A circle is made by taping (or sewing) together the two ends. Then the puppeteer can place the tip of a finger into the circle to manipulate the puppets. Older children enjoy these, and one person can manipulate several on one hand. They can be dressed up to denote any culture or type of person, or even an animal.

For paper finger puppets, draw a head and about half of the chest of the figure and color the picture. Include enough paper for the circle; then cut and tape together.

For felt finger puppets, cut pieces of felt 3 x 2½ inches for each puppet and sew up the side to make

a tube. The face and hair are drawn on a piece of construction paper ¾ x 2½ inches and glued onto the felt tube. Yarn can be added for hair, and a hat, if needed.

WHERE TO GET MORE HELP—

Tichenor, Tom, *Tom Tichenor's Puppets*. New York and Nashville: Abingdon Press, 1971. 219 pp. $5.95.

puzzles

WHAT THEY ARE—

Puzzles are problems or tasks done for fun that are set up in such a way that their solutions are usually found by using time, patience and one's ingenuity.

WHEN AND WHERE TO USE THEM—

Children can use puzzles at almost any time, often when amusing themselves. Certain types, especially word puzzles like crossword puzzles and acrostics, can also be used for review or summarizing at the end of a unit of study.

Puzzles can be used in any place where children are relaxing and having fun—in a car going on a trip, in a relaxing time at a day camp or summer camp, during an intergenerational experience at the church, or in the moments before a regular session begins in the child's classroom.

WHY CHILDREN USE THEM—

Puzzles allow children to:
—exercise the imagination and use mental abilities
—gain experience in succeeding in a problem-solving situation and in creating puzzles and problems for others to solve
—experience the challenge of coming up with solutions that are not readily apparent
—discover a new kind of fun and relaxation.

swimming duck

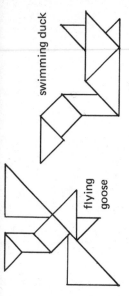

flying goose

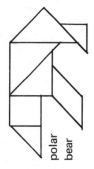

polar bear

baby chick

WHAT CHILDREN NEED—

—cardboard, wood
—onionskin or thin paper and pencil (for tracing)
—oak tag or cardboard
—teaching pictures
—white glue
—rolling pin or smooth curved jelly glass
—scissors, one-sided razor blades, or utility knife
—transparent self-stick plastic

HOW TO USE THEM—

Puzzles have an interesting history. A puzzle was found carved on the inside walls of the hollow head of the Sphinx, built in ancient Egypt. And more than 4000 years ago, the Chinese used as a pastime various figures formed from pieces of wood that could be rearranged.

Seek out many sources for puzzles for children. Evaluate commercial ones for their value in helping children learn and grow, as well as for enjoyment. Look in your local libraries for puzzle books and collections.

Children should also learn to develop puzzles, especially in relation to areas of interest or topics of study in which they have been involved.

The following are a few examples of puzzles that children enjoy.

The Tangram. The ancient Chinese made figures from seven pieces cut from a square of cardboard or wood. (See illustration)

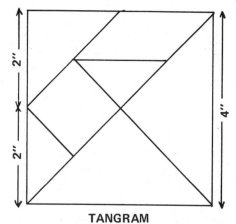

TANGRAM

All seven pieces must be used to make each figure, and none can overlap. The early Greeks had a similar puzzle with 14 pieces. A double tangram, it is cut from two squares the same size. Help children trace this puzzle with tissue paper and then cut one for themselves out of cardboard. Remember that these are nice gifts for boys and girls to give to friends. Encourage them to figure out some new solutions to both the single and double tangram puzzles.

Egg Puzzle. Prepare in the same way the six pieces shown below. These pieces can be fitted together to form an egg-shaped design.

Jigsaw Puzzles. For a simple jigsaw puzzle, glue a teaching picture or map on a piece of cardboard with white glue. Use a glass or rolling pin to get out all the air bubbles. When the picture is dry, mark on the back a design for cutting into puzzle pieces. Use sharp scissors or a one-sided razor blade or utility knife. If desired, the picture can also be covered with transparent self-sticking vinyl on one or both sides before cutting. For children younger than first grade, you may want to leave the outside frame together. This makes it easy for the small child to keep the puzzle together. For younger children make fewer and larger pieces.

Letter Ball. Trace this design and put it on cardboard or oak tag. It contains every letter of the alphabet. Why not encourage your older children to come up with a different design, making a puzzle containing all the numbers from 0 through 9. (See illustration, p. 126.)

solution

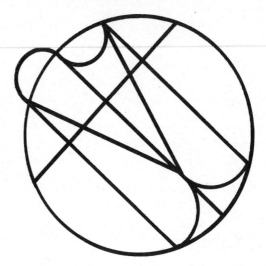

Trusting
Exciting
A
C
H
E
R
S

Word Puzzles. For one type of acrostic, place one main word down the left side of your paper. Then fill in words that begin with the letters used in the master word. Often the words incorporated into a given puzzle are related by subject matter—a season of the year, names, occupations, Bible people, etc. The example given here contains the beginnings of a word puzzle related to the master word, "teachers."

Box Words. These puzzles have words hidden in them (see illustration), and the object is to discover as many words as possible. Usually all the words in one puzzle center on one topic or theme.

Often puzzles like this are made up with spaces for twenty letters both across and down. Always the list

AMY   IRENE
JUNE   ELAINE
MARY   ANNABEL
RITA   ROBERTA
MABEL   MARGARET
SUSAN   VIRGINIA
HELEN

```
B G C E F I J D T V H
R U S T P E Y Z I P Q
B C D E F L P R Q T Y
O P T E R A G R A M O
Q R N W E I Z O A M O
S U S A N N A B E L J
J T U I V E E E W X Y
Z B A C D L F R G H I
I L P J O E N T I K M
R Y V U Q H S A W T X
I H C M J D E B Z O A
```

126

of hidden words is given, so that children can cross off or check each word as it is used.

Letters can be arranged so that correct answers can be spelled backwards or forward, up or down, or diagonally in any direction. (See illustration.)

The same letter may be used in more than one name, especially as the game progresses. Each time a word is found, the player draws a circle around it. Since the same letter may be used in more than one name, the circled areas may overlap. Be sure to mark off each word from the list as it is used.

Crossword Puzzles. Older elementary children can have fun making up as well as solving crossword puzzles. To make a puzzle, choose a list of words to use. Then block off a piece of paper with about 20 blocks across and 20 down.

Place one of the longer words in the middle of the puzzle. Then begin working out from that word by placing additional words that share a letter with it. Try to get the larger words in first and then work the smaller ones into smaller spaces by branching off from the larger words.

When all the words have been put in that seem to fit, shade the unused blocks. Then number the blocks containing letters, beginning at the top left hand corner and proceeding from left to right toward the bottom in each row.

When all letters, numbers and shaded blocks have been placed, make up a listing of definitions or clues for each word in the puzzle. Make a list for words going across and one for words going down, giving the number of the block where the first letter of each word is placed.

Sometimes children will become so adept at making puzzles that they can work them out in different shapes than the square design suggested here. Then the shading around the puzzle itself can be shaped to help indicate an overall design, such as a bird or animal or letter.

On the next page is a puzzle that has been started. Perhaps you will want to gain some experience by trying to finish it yourself.

See also Games.

CLUES TO CREATIVITY

Across

5	Large graceful water bird
9	
18	To move along in the water by arms or feet
22	A small vessel for water travel
32	A part of the face
36	
44	Moves from side to side or up and down
48	
57	
62	

71

Down

5	Abbr. for South West
6	Part of bird useful in flying
7	Prophet of Old Testament
9	
10	The openings in a fence
11	
13	
14	
22	Makers of honey
44	
45	
49	

These might be able to be worked in:

Toes	On
Tails	Igloo
Even	Claps
Vote or Voyage	Clip
SOS	School
	Trees